CU00971094

THE HE

LAKELAND

BY

LEHMANN J. OPPENHEIMER

TO

G. H. CRAIG

THE FRIEND WHO MOST SHARED IN AND OCCASIONED

THE ENJOYMENTS HEREIN DESCRIBED

This facsimile edition by
THE ERNEST PRESS

THE LATE LEHMANN J. OPPENHEIMER.

PREFACE.

THESE papers are concerned almost entirely with the wilder parts of Lakeland—the parts most loved by the mountaineer. Though written from a climber's point of view, I hope they will not be unintelligible to the much larger public which enjoys rambling amongst fine mountains without thinking of scaling their crags. Most of them were written years ago, and various changes have since taken place—not always for the better. More particularly I regret that one of the climbers introduced into the paper on " Wastdale Head at Easter " could not now justify his reference to the immunity of Lakeland from fatal climbing accidents. In 1899, when the paper first appeared in the *Climbers' Club Journal*, it was a fact, of which all frequenters of Wastdale Head were proud, that, in spite of the extreme difficulty of some of the climbs, and the great number of ascents—well over 10,000 I should estimate—which had been made up till then, no roped party had ever met with any serious accident in the district. Unhappily in 1903 a great catastrophe took place on Sca Fell, which destroyed our boast and robbed many of us of mountaineering friends.

Some note may seem called for respecting the undue prominence given to Buttermere. It must not be imagined that the proportion of space devoted to

PREFACE

the Buttermere climbs corresponds in any way with their relative claims to the climber's attention. I think far more highly of those at Wastdale, but they have been so well described by others that I have preferred to say little except about new ascents, and of these my friends and I have accomplished more at Buttermere than elsewhere.

The photographs must be considered rather as supplementing than illustrating the descriptions. The one of " Dawn amongst the Mountains " was taken in another district, but it is so like some dawns which I have seen in Lakeland, without having been able to photograph them, that I have been tempted to include it.

My thanks are due to the Editors of the *Manchester Quarterly* and of the *Climbers' Club, Fell and Rock Climbing Club* and *Rücksack Club Journals* for permission to reprint some of the papers.

LEHMANN J. OPPENHEIMER.

1908.

CONTENTS.

LIST OF ILLUSTRATIONS

Publisher's note;

As the author noted in the Preface to the First Edition, the photographs were supplementary to the text rather than complementing his descriptions. Therefore when some of the printed illustrations proved difficult to reproduce there was little hesitation about replacing them.

Accordingly Bob Allen kindly agreed to take his camera to specific sites and his photographs appear on pages 15, 63, 115, & 121. Geoff Milburn and Peter Hodgkiss also helped and theirs are the illustrations on pages 162 & 29 respectively.

Acknowledgement is also made to the Fell and Rock Climbing Club who kindly allowed reproduction of the portrait of Oppenheimer, his obituary in the special edition only and the map used to illustrate the chapter 'Buttermere as a climbing centre'.

I. EARLY IMPRESSIONS.

"Northwards." The mere thought of the word has a magical, invigorating power, even in the drowsy hours before dawn, when fellow-passengers are coiled in vain attempts at comfortable slumber. The feeling must be largely inspired by personal causes, for it can hardly come entirely from the nature of the northern country I love. I am not so blindly in love with it as to think that. Action, health-giving struggles with the elements and most of life's happiest moments are associated with it in my mind; and I can never enter a train northward-bound without thoughts clustering instinctively round Lakeland.

Wigan is passed with a sigh of relief, and I laugh to think how ideas change. In childhood, when my mother each summer took us to her Scotch home, Wigan was an enchanted town whose rows of signal lights and furnace flames licking up into the darkness were visions not to be missed. "Years have brought the inevitable yoke," and the place is no longer "apparelled in celestial light," but, with all their delusions, I look fondly back on those early journeys, for it was then that I learnt that love of the mountains which time has but confirmed, and which has become one of the most precious gifts of life.

How well I can see myself, as a child of six or seven, looking out with wide eyes for the Cheviots from the seat by the window. Very cautiously I clear the moisture from the glass at intervals, for my mother, though tired out and dozing, with one of my brothers asleep in her arms, is easily disturbed, and the least noise will make her sit up with a start and tell me to lie back and shut my eyes; so I gaze out in silence past the distracting fall and rise of the telegraph wires at the sleepy white villages strung along the high road, and the trees ankle-deep in mist flying by. For hours the same fields would seem to keep up with us, passed and yet ever recurring; then the first hints of light would appear over some low hills far away, and alternately I would be excited at the thought that we should soon be winding through the Cheviots, and weary at the slow march of the dawn and the endless, monotonous succession of trees and villages and telegraph poles, all as tiresome to me then as the unvarying rhythm of the rails beneath.

At length came Grayrigg Fells, or the Cheviots, as I thought them, for the mountains of England consisted in those days of three groups : the Pennines, often pointed out to me in the distance and despised; Sca Fell, Helvellyn and Skiddaw, three great isolated cones rising from a lake-dotted plain, watched for yearly but never knowingly seen; and the Cheviots, a range which neatly divided England from Scotland, and which consequently, I was bound to pass; the name I therefore attached to the most impressive hills seen on the journey. And very impressive these Grayrigg and Shap Fells were. At what an angle I had to look up to see their tops, silhouetted blue-grey against the dawn. Tiny sheep, dimly visible below, augmented the look of vastness, and as the train, whirling along the winding stream, leaned over towards the bulky shape, the slowness with which the mountain's form and position changed, increased the illusion. Then an opposing curve of the rails would sweep it away in a moment and bring fresh hills and hollows into view; over a coomb, at the head, a cloud brooded perhaps, turning the mountain grey to indigo and purple, and above in the higher air would be the first flush of pink amongst the pearly lights of morning. Those great stretches of moorland and mountain side, so beautiful in their loneliness, at once fascinated and frightened me; childish wonder passed into awe which intensified, until it was a relief to have the spell broken by someone straightening himself out and letting a sweet, cool draught into the stuffy carriage. Then what gladness to see the sun peer over the mountain rim, hiding it with an aureole of light—happily before it robbed the hills of their mystery they were far away from all but the eye of memory.

This eagerly-expected and long-remembered half-hour, yearly enjoyed, was the whole of my youthful acquaintance with mountains. I wonder will, my boy, who knew the lake hills before his alphabet, and has rambled over them with me when they have been wrapped in cloud, or laden with sunlit snow, in the clearness of May mornings and in hazy summer heat —will he, I wonder, when he grows up, long for the hills as I do, or will the rents his knickerbockers have sustained in his scrambles be the only outcome.

Curiously enough, I was never affected by the same hills seen in broad daylight on the return journey, nor yet by the grander distant mountains. To-day the attraction of Shap Fells is due mostly to the memories they call up, and much more precious is the far away little group of peaks seen across Morecambe Bay. As the train flies northward, leaving Kendal below, my eyes are now strained to disentangle the Pikes and Crinkles, and if perchance I recognise Mickledore in that small gap on the sky line, at once the Sca Fell cliffs rise in all their grandeur above it, and in place of the low, blue, ragged ridge, seen by the eye of childhood and sadly confirmed by the camera, groups of majestic peaks appear, separated by the most varied valleys— peaceful, luxuriant, romantic or desolate—and linked by grassy arms, with tarns lying lonely in the hollows of their outstretched hands. Thus is vision distorted by knowledge.

The knowledge was long in coming. Until after my schooldays were over I had never been amongst the hills, but at length I was allowed freedom, and the first use made of it was to hasten to the heart of Lakeland, the summit of Great Gable, to discover whether those blue shadowy hills were really grander than Grayrigg. I blush to think of this first scramble. Two-thirds of the way up the mountain I got on to screes lying at what seemed to me then an appalling angle, and with terror felt myself slipping. I believe I lay on the stones for a time, afraid to move lest the mountain should shiver down, taking me over the edge of one of the precipices. Screes in those days were frequently piled up until they stood 60 degrees from the horizontal, and they still seem able to maintain this angle in the work of amateur artists, though to anyone who knows the mountains well the effect is unconvincing; since they have been content with an inclination of 35 to 40 degrees their terrors have vanished. The precipices also seem to have decreased in number, and instead of perpetually yawning beneath the mountain rambler they have of late years required some hunting. The fright occasioned by this little episode was soon banished by the delight of being for the first time on a mountain top. The freedom was what impressed me most; mile upon mile of wild country over which one could wander at will. It made me whirl my arms over my head in idiotic ecstacy. What joy to be able to cast off all restraint, to feel far out of anyone's sight or hearing, alone with Nature. I shouted, and was startled at the stillness; rushed about over the boulders to dissipate a nervous tremble caused by the strange loneliness, and came unexpectedly to the edge overlooking Wastdale and

Hell Gate. Then for the first time I appreciated the austere grandeur of the mountains; of the mountains themselves, apart from adventitious aid of dawn or cloud or sunset glow. The Napes ridges proudly rearing up below me and the screes shooting down to the feet of those great rocks, sinuously swathing them, passing through their narrow gates and then down, far below, with unswerving straightness towards the distant stream—these filled me with new feelings of wonder.

But freedom was still the greatest discovery, and day after day, holiday after holiday, I returned to seek out the wildest fells, happy if rid of fields and fences, moving my quarters daily as desire guided, without the shackles of a plan. I began to feel that my mountain novitiate was over, and imagined that I enjoyed the hills to the full. As a matter of fact, I could not truly appreciate their very grandest parts. I often sat by Sprinkling Tarn to admire Great End; most of the cliffs in the district I had seen, but for over a dozen years I saw them with only half-opened eyes. Since I began to climb them they have been charged with quite a new impressiveness, even viewed from below or in the distance. I could not have believed, in those earlier days, that an intense appreciation of the mountains might be compatible with the most undignified gymnastics upon them, or that hilarious levity brimming over from jovial companions might even enhance the wild beauty of gullies and ridges; but experience has taught me that scenery is enjoyed most in pauses between muscular and mental efforts. You are climbing a difficult chimney; your whole attention is given to surmounting the chock-stone just above, you wedge your knees firmly, your fingers manage to grip the stone, then a few moments of violent exertion and you are up. While you are recovering breath before looking after the rope for the next man the whole picture flashes into your mind and stamps itself there in a way that rarely happens when you look long and intently, trying to stamp it there yourself. Or you are sketching; while intent on reproducing the tones and colours of a sombre evening a filmy cloud on the mountain verge is suddenly seized by the hidden sun and turned to a fringe of fire; it sends down streamers into the shadow, leaves them to wind stealthily in the cold, round unsuspected pinnacles, and floats away, a mass of glowing vapour, reflecting radiance, as it moves, on to the slabs of rock in the dark hollow beneath. You feel mad at the hopelessness of altering your sketch, but in those few moments before the gold is dimmed and the grey prevails, you will have drunk in more enjoyment than ever you would if you had merely gone out to watch the sunset. I have often heard that the best way to enjoy river scenery is to go fishing, and I feel confident that no greater opportunities to appreciate mountain grandeur are afforded than in climbing one of the grey cliffs which so often gather round the nobler summits.

But the best gift of the mountains to me came before I thought of rock-climbing; it may not be found by seeking; like joy, it is oftenest attained when on some other quest; follow it and it will fly away.

> Who takes no thought
> To him 'tis brought
> To him, unsought 'tis given.

I myself gained it in suffering, and the recollection is still painful. I well remember stamping about on the Gable top all night, heedless alike of its grandeur and the cold. It was the most terrible night I have had to endure, a night of mental torture. Slowly the dark hours passed by, but before morning the spell of the hills had wrought its work. Since that day the mountains have been more to me than mere playgrounds; from majestic piles of grass- or lichen-covered rocks they were transformed to titans, who in their dreams listen to the joys and woes of the little restless wanderers amongst them, still them and echo their emotions in after years, returning the sweets of sorrow without its bitterness. From that night I have understood Coleridge's lines:

> O Lady! we receive but what we give
> And in our life alone does nature live:
> Ours is her wedding-garment, ours her shroud!
>   And would we aught behold, of higher worth,
> Than that inanimate cold world allowed
> To the poor loveless ever-anxious crowd,
>   Ah, from the soul itself must issue forth
> A light, a glory, a fair luminous cloud
>   Enveloping the Earth.

But the life with which Lakeland is now invested by experience, apart from this one strain of sorrow, is wholly joyous. Derwentwater and Patterdale have always their " wedding garments " and rejoice in the memory of roses. Langdale, too, is always the valley of friendship; Bow Fell may be storm-enveloped or snow-clad, but I still see it as on that June morning when two hardy ramblers came upon me endeavouring to paint the mists travelling up its hollows; a chance meeting, amongst the hills, of three who had lived close to one another for years without getting beyond nods and commonplaces. What times we have had together since, what tramps over moor and mountain, what memorable days on the Pillar, what sights for the gods ! For years we have religiously observed the principal festivals, appointed by the Church, in Lakeland, feasting the day long in our own fashion " under the canopy," and returning nightly to make merry over flagons of shandygaff at the Wastdale or Buttermere inn.

Experiences have all endeared the district to me, so that I perhaps have an exaggerated idea of its loveliness, but remembrance of even the greater glories of Switzerland does but heighten its beauty for me. There is a delightful quietness about it all; no straining after startling effects like that of the Eiger, no " canine tooth in a gigantic carnivorous jaw," as Mr. Dent has called the Dru; even the Langdale Pikes, the nearest approach to the bizarre, look broadly based and strongly buttressed, and the little farms nestle comfortably at their feet. Nay, even under the grey cliffs of Sca Fell, silent, but for the drip of water from its high overhanging walls and the lonely call of the raven, out of sight of field or farm you are conscious that this spot of central wildness is girt round by the most habitable of mountain regions. Small—in a day it can be crossed in any direction—yet containing as many different types of beauty as it has valleys, and each type ever varying in mood. Time may perhaps, through the ruthless hand of man, wither certain charms; but, as was said about Cleopatra of old, custom can never stale its infinite variety.

And now this very personal prelude is over, and those who have found no echo of my mountain apprenticeship in their own memories may give a sigh of relief and pass on to scenes and doings well-known to lovers of Lakeland.

AFTERNOON SUN ON GABLE CRAG

SCA FELL FROM LINGMELL

II. WASTDALE HEAD AT EASTER.

ALTHOUGH Wastdale lies at the foot of the grandest hills in England and only a few miles from crowded tourist centres, there are few spots of equal beauty so undisturbed by traffic, noise, and other accompaniments of a civilization to which too many holiday resorts have fallen victims. As yet no signboards point the way to the best scenery, the waterfalls are unenclosed, and the mountain sides undesecrated by railways. Many a day have I spent rambling with an ecstatic sense of perfect freedom over Great Gable and Sca Fell, seeing no one from morning till dusk, and hearing only the far away roar of the becks below, or the shivering clatter of scree beneath my feet. Yet if anyone should go to Wastdale at Easter hoping to enjoy the mountain solitude—" the sleep that is amongst the lonely hills "—though other, and unexpected enjoyments may be thrust upon him, in his hope he is likely to be disappointed.

As he nears the hotel, hungry and tired after a night in the train and a walk of a dozen miles from the coast, he hears an unwonted hum of voices, and entering the yard he finds a group looking up at, and shouting to a man who seems stuck like a fly some ten feet up the rough wall of the barn, feeling with one hand amongst the open joints of the stonework

for a hold higher up. He stares a little at these
antics, but being on the wrong side of breakfast he
wastes no time and passes on to more important
business. From the hall he catches sight of the
innkeeper's daughter passing from the kitchen to the
coffee room with a huge dish of ham and eggs, and
shouts out, " Good morning ! Can you give me a
room for a few days and something to eat at once."

" I'm afraid not, sir," she says shyly, and glides
past into the room.

" What ! I can't have breakfast ! What's the
meaning of this ?" he asks in astonishment, following
her to the door. " As I'm alive some day-trippers
have forestalled me and taken possession of the
place. What a rough lot they look—what a
pandemonium." He waits to waylay the lassie as
she returns with a pile of empty porridge plates, but
meanwhile the kitchen door opens again and a fine
old fellow with the face and gait of a Cumberland
shepherd appears. " Ah ! Good day, Mr. Tyson.
I wanted breakfast and a room for a few nights, but it
seems doubtful whether my wants can be satisfied."

" Eh, sir ! Every room in the house was taken
two or three weeks ago ; there's some folk sleepin'
i'the smoke-room and some i'the barn—not a bed to
spare nowhere, and they are full up at Burnthwaite
too."

" How provoking. I've often been here before in
the height of the season and never had any difficulty
in getting a room ; I thought at this time of the year

I should almost have the place to myself. Some
trip from Barrow or Whitehaven, eh?"

" Eh, no : there's only a two three gentlemen fro'
these parts : mostly they're from all over England—
London and Oxford, and Yorkshire and Manchester,
and I dunno wheere all : they come up every
Eastertide, a lot of 'em—a daft lot. But there'll be
a second breakfast presently—there are some
hangin' about outside waitin' for it."

At this moment a wild-looking unshaven individual
enters, without collar or tie, and with knickerbockers
well torn and patched; he gazes abstractedly at the
traveller and passes on into the coffee-room.

" Who in the world is that Bohemian?" our friend
asks.

"Oh, he comes fro' some place down i'the South—
ay, Cambridge they call it—they say he writes verses
and plays, but I dunno much about that sort o' thing.
An awful clever sort o' chap, but ye can never mak'
out what he's drivin' at. There are some comin' out
now; they'll have finished, so if you'r wantin' summat
to eat you'd better get a seat afore some other body
comes in."

Breakfast is proceeding merrily : the talk at the
table is loud and jovial, for the majority in the room
have met at least half of those present before, either
here or at Pen-y-Gwryd or amongst the Alps, and
have plenty of tales to tell and experiences to
compare. The Bohemian combs his hair with his
fingers before joining the company, which, however,

seems hardly to expect such a work of supererogation from him. Only three very proper young men, with well-starched collars and cuffs, turn and look up with wonder as he takes a vacated seat next to them, one dropping the lower lip slightly and another raising an eye-glass. But indeed he is not the only unconventional figure at table. Most of the others wear jerseys or coarse flannel shirts without collars : some are breakfasting without their jackets which are still at the fire recovering from the vicissitudes of the previous day. The only one whose attire can be called dainty is the Christ Church undergraduate. He wears a white flannel shirt fastened by a silk cord with tassels instead of a stud, and he has no waistcoat to hide the hardly visible white embroidery down the front. The patches on his jacket have been so carefully sewn on as to be inconspicuous. His watch is carried for safety in a small leathern pouch fastened to his belt, but he is careless enough to wear and endanger the beauty of an exquisite Greek cameo set in a ring of Venetian workmanship, for the scars on the back of his hands show that he has had plenty of close acquaintance with the rocks. He and the Bohemian represent opposite tastes in the matter of dress, but though extremes in appearance, in higher things they meet.

Much of the conversation at breakfast takes the form of speculation or prophecy : various parties are inquiring how much the barometer has fallen and discussing whether the day will be better for rocks

or snow, ridges or gullies.   Presently the three
faultlessly dressed ones retire.   " Do you think
those men are climbers?" the Bohemian asks loudly,
looking round the room with affected doubt in his
face, amidst roars of laughter.   " I merely ask," he
continues, " to acquire information, and seeing that
they display some interest in the subject.   One of
them made some inquiries about the lunatic who was
performing on the wall outside, meaning I presume
our friend the photographer doing the barn-door
traverse."

    " It's like you to call me names in that underhand
way," replies the photographer, ' but we're in the
same boat you know—' the lunatic, the lover, and the
poet,' as your friend says."

    " Do I look like a lover?" the Bohemian asks with
feigned simplicity.

    " Oh, you're not going to entice me into flattering
you by saying you look like a poet."

    Several men now move off, laughing as they go.
The room is gradually emptying.   The Yorkshire
party has been in earnest over breakfast, hardly
stopping to talk, but the Christ Church man, though
one of the first down, is still dallying with his knife
and chatting with a member of the Alpine Club.   " I
must confess," the latter is saying, " that I like these
little English climbing expeditions better in many
ways than the Swiss ones.   A good English breakfast and a night's rest at the back of it are delights to
begin with.   You go out into the fresh morning air

readier to enjoy the mountains than after having been rudely wakened at one or two at night, sitting down cold and half asleep to a roll and cup of coffee, and tramping for an hour or two along interminable moraines and glaciers by the feeble light of a candle."

" But then think," replies the undergraduate, " of sitting down to breakfast at dawn amongst the snows; the solemnity and stillness of it all : the great Alps towering above in sunlight through the mists of the morning, to say nothing of the meat and wine and raisins and honey, tasting as food never tasted in an hotel."

" Oh yes! I grant all that : I don't mean what I said quite seriously of course; but at the same time there are certain enjoyments connected with English climbing that you don't get amongst the Alps, and do you know, too, I think that whilst there isn't the hundredth part of the danger the standard of difficulty is higher here."

" Oh, how can you say so?" the Christ Church man ejaculates.

" Well of course I know that any of the English mountains could be climbed by a boy of six or seven if he took the easiest way as people do amongst the Alps, but a different system prevails here; the difficulties are hunted for, and in misty weather often can't be found. You've been up the Grépon, haven't you?"

" Yes, I climbed it with our Oriel friend last summer."

" Well, there you have one of the stiffest Chamounix climbs, but it's hardly as difficult as the end gully on the Screes, or Kern Knotts Crack, or half-a-dozen other recognised ascents here."

" I am afraid you have me in a corner now, for I was beaten by Kern Knotts Crack only yesterday; still I won't give in, because there are more than mere gymnastic difficulties in the Alps. No, to my mind the only great advantage that England has over Switzerland is the absence of the professional element."

" Well as far as that goes you needn't take guides unless you wish."

" That may be all right for you after all your experience," replies the undergraduate, " I wouldn't like to attempt it; but there is a great charm about the compulsory reliance of two or three firm friends on each other here. I shall feel far more delight if we succeed in getting up the crack to-day by ourselves than if Simond or Burgener led the way."

How long this conversation will continue seems doubtful : the room is becoming deserted, and we will follow the deserters into the hall. In it stand three pairs of well-blacked shining boots, and some forty or fifty others streaming with oil; strong and heavy, the soles and heels completely surrounded by curiously shaped nails. All the men who can crush into the little standing room left are trying to

discover their belongings : outside some are hammer-
ing fresh nails into gaps made the previous day, and
on the stairs others are attempting to extricate their
ropes from the many which wind up the staircase,
strained tight round the newel posts, reminding one
of Wordsworth's yews :—

> A growth
> Of intertwisted fibres serpentine
> Up-coiling, and inveterately convolved.

In groups of two, three, four or five the climbers
stroll off with their ropes and ice-axes, and their
pockets swollen with lunch.   A couple of hours
more and the cliffs of Sca Fell and Great Gable will
be ringing with voices and the hotel will have
resumed its wonted quietness.   Our disappointed
friend has departed with his knapsack to try for
better luck at Rosthwaite, and the three tourists
attired in mackintoshes, are wandering along the
road towards the lake.

"Well, I'm awfully glad to get away from those
rowdy fellows," says the man with the eye-glass.

These tourists look wonderfully alike at the first
glance : they have all such a monotonous air of
conventional respectability about them, but their
uniformity is merely superficial.   The most sensitive
and æsthetic of them is revelling in the scenery and
longing for some expression of appreciation from his
companions.   Half-way down the lake they turn
and stand long looking back at Great Gable.   "What
a splendidly buttressed pyramid the Gable is," he

says, " and just look at those clouds blowing along between its peak and those sharp rocky teeth just beneath it."

The bumptious little tourist puts up his eye-glass. " Yes, awfully jolly, isn't it?—that's where those fellows at the hotel must be : I asked one of them where that awful looking rock was that there are so many photographs of in the dining-room, and he told me it was up there. They'll be getting drenched in the cloud and seeing nothing : I'm blessed if I can imagine where the fun comes in : there can't be much enjoyment in fagging up those insane places in the wet."

" Brag, sir ! merely brag—that, I have no doubt, is their enjoyment," adds the eldest of the three.

" Do you see that faint line across the mountain, lower down?" asks their friend.

" Well, what of it?"

" That's the path Gray writes about in one of those letters that are so much ridiculed to-day. He tells about coming up Borrowdale under the guidance of someone who informed him that beyond Seathwaite all access was barred to prying mortals : there was only a dreadful track, impassable except by the hardy dalesmen, and open to them but for a few weeks in the year."

" What rot ! Why the gentleman we left at the hotel was going that way with quite a heavy knap-sack : those old chaps talked a lot of nonsense about the hills : they didn't believe what they said—not tney : I expect they wanted to show off a bit about the terrible places they'd been to."

" I'm not so sure about that : mountains seem to exercise a very disturbing influence on our accurate observation of fact even now, and I believe they had a much greater effect in times past. I rather think our susceptibilities are getting blunted to our great loss. Why have we come here now? Simply because we wanted something grander and more impressive than the scenes round Derwentwater and Windermere : we have got so accustomed to the hills there that we begin to think them a little tame. Well, as far as I am concerned, I wish I could take Gray's place, enjoying all the luxuriant beauty of Keswick and Ambleside, and yet imagining the scenery there to be also savage and sublime, the cliffs impending and threatening to overwhelm, and the roads only not perpendicular. At least I'm glad that the view before us satisfies my craving for grandeur, and that I haven't to risk my neck with those climbers in order to find it."

The elder tourist, somewhat uncommunicative as a rule, adds, as if to settle the point, " No one could find it in such company—men struggling to degenerate into apes."

" How do you make that out?" asks the little man.

" Well it is generally admitted that the hands and feet of infants are peculiarly adapted for climbing—"

" What's that got to do with it? You're going to prove we ought all to be climbers."

" My dear sir, as I was about to remark, these
adaptations are vestigial ; they indicate our ancestry :
as we develop they become imperfect ; the anthropoid
ape in man tends to disappear ; but those fellows at
the hotel won't let it die, they attempt to return to a
stage that is past."

" By Jove ! I must play that card off on someone
at dinner-time.   Oh ! I say ! rain again—what an
infernal nuisance—let's turn and make for lunch."

This and many other things I hear and see, in
imagination, as I plod with two friends up the breast
of Lingmell, leaving conversation for flatter ground :
but at last the shoulder of the hill is turned and the
tourists forgotten as we stand gazing at the sunshine
far away over the sea, and the solemn purple gloom
of the Mosedale amphitheatre of mountains.   The
cliffs whither we are bound are still hidden from
view,

In fleecy cloud voluminous enwrapped,

but we can see the base of the great precipice, and
that is enough to call up visions of the happy days we
have spent on it, and to make our hearts leap with
joyful anticipation.   A mile more of easy tramping
up a grassy tongue between chattering becks, then a
scramble up the scree-shoot that comes down from
Lord's Rake, and we are at the foot of the cliff
whose top is Sca Fell Pinnacle.   Here we have a
rest and a smoke, sitting where we can look up into
Deep Gill, and watch the snow gleaming weirdly

through the mist, high up the gully, like a phantom light between its dark dripping walls.

At last we rouse ourselves to action, tie on the rope, sling the ice-axes over our wrists, and start clambering slowly round and up the base of the precipice into Steep Gill.   Soon we are in the cloud, but the dampness is a trifle compared with the drenching we get from the rocks.   We pull ourselves up cautiously on to a ledge, and the water trickles down both sleeves; we back up a narrow chimney and are suddenly aware of a cold sensation about the patched part of our trousers, and finally we grow callous.   Then comes some step-cutting up the snow in Steep Gill, followed by a traverse out again on to the face of the cliff.   The ascent admits of fewer variations as we reach this part, and we are led to an exposed shelf beyond which all further traversing seems impossible.   Our way from here appears to be straight up : ten or twelve feet above the shelf starts a fine-looking chimney which leads to the top : but how to reach the foot of it?   The ledge we are on is the top of a great block, separated from the main mass of the cliff by a fissure a foot wide and of great depth : on the other side of this fissure the rock rises steeply, and with very slight holds, to the foot of the chimney.   Instead of tackling it at once we all three, finding the shelf just large enough, sit down on it with our backs to the difficulty, and for a while watch the cloud whirling round and below us. One of my companions is a strong, broad-shouldered, cautious fellow; he is appreciating the scene round our airy perch to the full, but he says nothing about it : the other is somewhat of a contrast. He is wiry and six feet three high; beside him I feel but a dwarf, and he has a reach long even in proportion to his height. It is a pleasure merely to watch him striding away over the mountains with his cap stuffed into his pocket and his face brimming over with delight. Whatever strikes him he says straight out, and he often expresses for us what we all feel. As we sit on our perilous ledge suddenly some huge dark object appears moving steadily towards us. For a moment a shiver runs through us; then an exultant thrill and my tall friend shouts out, ' Oh, man ! how grand it is to be alive !" The cloud is dispersing and the vague shape of terror is resolving itself into the cliffs on the opposite side of Mickledore. A patch of blue sky follows and presently there is sunshine on all the mountains round. Thin clouds form and trail and vanish again below us, and we hasten to get out of the shadow of the great cliff and into the warmth ourselves.

The difficulty proves by no means as serious as it looked. We hitch the rope round a knob of rock in case of a slip, and steady the tall man as he reaches a high handhold on the opposite side of the cleft and struggles into a place of security. Then we join him, give him a shoulder to reach the foot of the chimney and follow him up it to the lower peak of the pinnacle. Here we are in full view of the top, to which the Low Man is joined by a rib some fifty feet long, like an acute roof ridge tilted up at one end. This is the most sensational piece of the ascent, and at the same time the easiest. The ridge has to be crossed straddle-wise, one leg pointing down right into Steep Gill and the other into Deep Gill. Then comes a scramble over some broken rocks and at last we are on the summit of the Pinnacle.

Here, in one of the grandest spots in England, with the snows and rocks of the Sca Fell chasms beneath us on either hand, a tumult of mountains round us, and a distance of fertile valleys, glistening lakes and azure sea, our first thought is, sad to confess, of lunch. Pockets are soon emptied : bread and butter, potted meat, raisins, prunes, chocolate, crystallised ginger and brandy—a queer mixture truly, and no doubt the three tourists lunching quietly at the hotel would have pitied us as much as we pitied them. As I am spreading the potted meat on the bread and butter with my penknife our tall friend says, " I wonder if either of you remember an old picture by Tenniel of a large modern plate-glass window, filled with tinned fruits and potted meats; outside, Romeo in antique garb, is looking wistfully at the nineteenth-century grocer's stock, and below is the legend :

> An' if a man did need a poison now,
> Here lives a caitiff wretch would sell it him.

SCA FELL PINNACLE.

WASTDALE HEAD HOTEL.

" However," he says, taking a large bite, " after your trouble in bringing the pot up that chimney I'll do my duty at all risks.   Here's to you, grand old pinnacle !   But let's bury the pot under a stone and pick up our silver paper."

" What ho !" shouts a familiar voice, and, turning round, we see the merry face of the Photographer appearing over the edge of the rocks on Sca Fell itself, followed rapidly by four others.

" Another first ascent ?" we shout back inquiringly.

" Not to-day; we've been in Moss Gill taking the direct finish; none of the others had tried it.   Which way have you come?   Steep Gill?   Grand fun along the arête, isn't it?   You know there's a new way now to the ledge below Slingsby's chimney? O. G. found it out.   Right up the angle of the cliff."

The Photographer's knowledge of the crags is most amazing; not only every climb but every variation seems familiar to him.   His party is a right jovial one, and, finishing our lunch, we descend from the Pinnacle by the " easy way " to join it.

" How are the mighty fallen."   Before Haskett Smith made the first ascent a shepherd was asked if he thought such a feat possible.

" Eh, mon," he said, " nobbut a fleein' thing 'll ever get up theer !"

Now it is the " easy way," and which is the difficult one there is no telling for any length of time.   Until six years ago the route by which we have just ascended held the place of honour, and now there is some doubt whether the one that then displaced it has not fallen in its turn. Soon those anxious to make ascents in new ways will have to adopt the tactics of an old hand at the game, who last year succeeded in climbing a famous boulder, near Wastdale, feet uppermost.

By the time we have descended from the Pinnacle another party has joined the Moss Gill group, and Sca Fell presents a lively scene. My two friends suddenly start a wrestling match in memory of Professor Wilson. One of the Photographer's companions bursts into song, and the Photographer himself tells us all kinds of stories about famous climbers who have been here.

At last we separate, and our party makes off for Mickledore Chimney : we drop over the top blocks and cautiously cut steps downwards in the hard snow and ice with which the gully is choked. Lower down the snow is softer, and the leader, steadied by the rope above, can kick holes for the feet, and as we near the bottom we indulge in a glissade. This proves so intoxicating that the strong man of the party, after unroping, rushes some way up the chimney, again and again, to enjoy the exhilaration of the rapid descent. Time after time he plunges up the snow, each time going a little higher and whizzing down more rapidly, until at last he loses his balance and ungracefully rolls over into the scree below amidst the laughter of less energetic onlookers. After this he thinks it might be well to sit on

Mickledore Ridge and watch other mountaineers for a while, so we lazily look on at the desperate but futile efforts of two men to get up the first few feet of the great climb on the face of Sca Fell cliffs. We tried the same thing ourselves for an hour the day before, so we take an envious interest in their struggles, and, our vanity being soothed by their defeat, we go round to show them a way of circumventing the difficulty, invented by the Photographer.

On our way back to the hotel the tall man insists on our trying a few first ascents of our own on some fine-looking boulders, and by the time Wastdale Head is reached we are warm and damp and dirty and hungry enough to think of nothing but cold water, dry clothes, and dinner.

Several parties have returned and are lolling about in the hall waiting for the sound of the gong. As we sit down on the stairs to take off our boots the Bohemian walks in with his companions, remarking to the company at large :

" ' My knees are weak through fasting; and my flesh faileth of fatness.' ' Bring me a cup of sack ! ' Good Lord ! what two fools belong to those laths in the hat-rack? Bamboo alpenstocks !—tin ferrules tacked on to look like spikes—spiral coil of summits burnt in and varnished at half a franc a-piece."

" Don't talk so loud, old chap ! They're just in the smoke-room round the corner."

" Grindlewald, 3,468 feet," the Bohemian shouts; " a noble peak to start with—Wengern Alp, 6,184—

how I can see them ascending by the cog-wheel railway—Pilatus—Righi—Stanserhorn ——— " we hear him proclaiming down below as we make for our rooms to prepare for dinner.

At last the gong sounds and the dining-room is rapidly filled. With what eager expectant faces all the company await the soup; everyone has plenty to tell of what the day has brought forth, but talk is not free until the first course is over; then the ring of voices rises and dinner slowly proceeds to the accompaniment of a merry clamour of tongues.

The Bohemian has donned a tie and combed his hair, and the three faultlessly-attired tourists begin to look on him as a fellow man. He first addresses my neighbour across the table :

" Pray have you seen two most egregious swells with lofty bamboo sticks? "

" Oh, those men with the marvellous alpenstocks? Yes, I saw them leaving the hotel in a trap shortly before dinner."

" Aha ! I am glad of it—their accent was of ' Stratford-atte-Bowe,' and I hold with old Christopher North that although a cat may look at a king, a Cockney should not be allowed to look at a mountain."

" I suppose there were lively times at Wastdale when Christopher North descended on it," says the literary touirst, anxious to get on to safer ground. " I once read an account of his pranks here in a book of Edwin Waugh's."

" You observe that grey-haired old boy making yawning gaps in a leg of mutton? Ask him. A Liverpool doctor—used to come here forty years ago, and knew Will Ritson well. ' Verily,' he will say, ' the former days were better than these.' ' Foolhardy gymnastics,' he calls our kind of climbing; but he tramps all over the mountains to watch us. If you want to know about Wilson and Tyson and Ritson and the days that are past, ask him."

" What sort of a man was Ritson? "

" Behold his portrait at the end of the room, with his clay pipe and mug of beer; the man who boasted that Wastdale had the highest mountain, deepest lake, smallest church, and biggest liar in England."

" Indeed ! " remarks the tourist, " I've heard before of the first three, though the third is disputed, but never of the fourth. Who is he? "

" Why, Ritson himself of course, while he lived; and though he is dead, Wastdale still maintains her supremacy. You will be convinced after dinner, when you have heard the stories that will be told—climbing with teeth and eye-lashes—sticking on to seamless perpendicular cliffs by the mere friction of tweed trousers—"

" Well, after looking at the photographs round these walls I am ready to believe almost anything. By the way, you seem to have been trying to stick on to a cliff by the friction of the back of your hand : I hope you haven't injured yourself."

" A mere scrape—I foolishly jammed it in a crack—the smart is trifling and ' the labour we delight in physics pain.' "

" That was not what you said at the time " interrupts the gentleman on the other side of the Bohemian.

" I probably said ' Damn,' " he replies.

" I would have respected you more if you had : as far as I remember you said ' Verily my flesh is consumed away that it cannot be seen, and my bones that were not seen stick out.' "

" You probably don't remember how that most apt utterance was followed by a noise as of ' the crackling of thorns under a pot.' "

" Oh ! I admit that we were not very sympathetic, but it was too ridiculous to watch your pretended indifference to the scrape until you had got out your inevitable quotation."

" How appropriately, from your point of view, this room is decorated," the tourist continues after the interruption, " you have photographs of all your climbs round the walls to refer to, you have Ritson at the end to remind you of—"

" Yes, and a card at the other end to remind you that you may not smoke in this room, which is not appropriate from my point of view : but you'll see we'll remove the obnoxious document after dinner " the Bohemian adds.

" While you are talking of appropriate decorations " the laconic elder tourist hastens to interject

" don't forget the portrait hanging in the place of honour, looking down between those needles and cliffs and gullies like the corpse at an Egyptian feast: a powerful sermon, but you are all heedless of what it—"

" Sir, will you dare to say that if the Professor could come back to us he would not approve—"

" No, no, no—I don't want you to take it that way: I know he had the climbing fever and that it wasn't whilst climbing that he was so unfortunately killed. I spoke with an eye on my friend here: I am afraid he is being seduced by the prevailing enthusiasm, and I wished to remind him that there is ' mountain gloom ' as well as ' mountain glory.' "

The Bohemian regards him with scorn, saying

' Cowards die many times before their deaths;
    The valiant never taste of death but once.'

Dinner over, the company is scattered about the Hotel, yet every room seems crowded. Some remain in the dining-room, discussing the possibility of new ascents with the aid of the large photographs on the walls. In the smoke room the sofa and chairs are all occupied and several men are lying on the floor round the fire, leaning against other people's legs, renewing the adventures of the day and garnishing Swiss experiences of the summer before with lively flights of imagination. The veterans have a stock of stories about their various guides and every exploit recounted suggests to someone else another, still more thrilling, humourous or improbable. As coffee is passed round and the room fills with smoke criticism slumbers: the narratives become more imaginative and relate to far off periods: jokes from Leslie Stephen and Mummery pass as original and raise a laugh for the hundredth time, and gradually the company settles down into a blissful dreamy state, thinking lazily of past victories and defeats that rise and pass and fade with the flickerings of the fire.

Meanwhile the more energetic may be found in the billiard room, shouting and laughing as the ball rebounds or flies off the table to the imminent danger of someone's head. " By Jove, what a game! No wonder we couldn't play this afternoon " the bumptious little tourist remarks to his laconic friend, " the ball must be covered with notches." The table is being used for a game of fives and the partners are rushing wildly backwards or forwards, or into their opponents. The Bohemian stops to take off his coat—" Not that I love warmth less, but freedom more." And now yet oftener the ivory ball flies off and adds to its many dinges, until at last a collision between it and an enthusiastic spectator suggests a change. " Let's have the passage of the billiard table leg." This is a well known feat and all congregate round a corner of the table to watch one after another make the attempt. Only the gymnast succeeds: he begins by sitting on the table, despite the warning notice above him of a half-crown fine for such an offence; he lets himself down gently, and, suddenly twisting round, he braces his legs firmly against the cross-bars underneath; from above nothing can now be seen of him but one hand clutching the cushion, but all are watching down below to see that he does not touch the ground.   After a struggle his other hand and his head appear on the opposite side of the table leg, and a moment afterwards he is sitting breathless on the table once more, amidst loud cheers.   Then the respective advantages of tall and short men in climbing are discussed, and the heights and reaches of all in the room are marked on the wall.   Next the billiard room traverse is suggested, but no one responds.   After much pressing the gymnast consents to try.   He takes off his coat and shoes, and placing his hands on the edge of the billiard table he walks backwards up the wall to within a yard of the ceiling.   Then he moves along the table and wall simultaneously with hands and feet, avoiding the framed chromolithographs as well as he may.   With an enormous stride he reaches from one wall to another at the corner of the room, and is just saved from upsetting some half-emptied glases of whisky on the mantelshelf by the terrified shouts of the owners.   The next corner is easier, and in the middle of the third wall he can rest his legs awhile on the window ledge.   The fourth wall is more difficult again : it contains a large recess, too deep to reach from the billiard table and only a foot lower than the ceiling. All round the angle of this he must pass before he arrives at the door, which is set diagonally across the corner of the room. This is the *mauvais pas* of the performance. The gymnast cautiously brings one foot down until his toe rests on the latch hold; then, supporting himself from the corner of the billiard table with one hand, he reaches the top of the door lintel with the other, lets go with the first, swings round in the opening and catches the lintel on the opposite side also. Here he gets the first rest for his arms by jamming himself tightly in the opening with his back and legs. To complete the traverse in the orthodox way he has still to work along the passage as far as to the smoke room, and this, after an uncomfortable rest, he quickly does with back against one wall and feet against the other, finally opening the smoke room door and descending to terra firma. The tales and visions of the company there assembled are interrupted by cheers, and those who have missed the performance unreasonably clamour for a repetition. An old hand insidiously suggests that there are three variations of the move into the doorway, and the gymnast is dragged back once more to try them. Then there are tests of balance, of hanging on the rope and lifting people with it, of wriggling through narrow chair backs, and the evening wears away in attempting or watching all kinds of mad antics.

Outside, in the cold clear starlight, the literary

tourist, having deserted his two companions, is walking up and down with the Oxford man, looking up in reverent silence at the dark silhouette of Great Gable, or discussing how best to enter into the spirit of the mountains.

" My own experience," the undergraduate says, " leads me to think that only by spending the night alone on the fell tops can you fully enjoy the grandeur and solemnity and the weird mystery of the mountains."

" If you feel so why do you desecrate them by climbing about in their most secret recesses with those noisy fellows inside?   I myself have at times felt a very strong inclination to climb amongst the rocks, but I have always been deterred by the thought of approaching them in such company— and perhaps by the danger that everyone talks about. I would like to go alone but I am too afraid of getting into a fix."

" Well, do you know, you cannot have every kind of pleasure at once : there are joys of exertion and victory, and of jovial company, as well as of meditation amongst the lonely hills.   As to the danger, I am afraid a very exaggerated idea of it prevails.   Many people have certainly been killed on these fells and I would not advise you to go rock climbing alone, but no serious accident has yet happened in the Lake District to any properly roped party, and a great amount of climbing is done here. I remember when I was a boy hearing that not half-a-dozen people had ever reached the top of the famous Pillar in Ennerdale; that there was only one way, and it was necessary to start with a particular foot first, for if you failed to do this you arrived at a difficult corner in such a position as not to be able to advance or retire. Well, of course this was all nonsense : there were at least six routes known even then, and plenty of people climbed it. Now there are nine principal ways and many variations : I should think over a hundred ascents are made every year, many of them by the long and difficult routes on the North face, so you may feel assured that the danger is not so considerable. Will you come there with us to-morrow? I am sure you would enjoy it. The views are grand, every muscle will be called into action, ingenuity has to be exercised continually to overcome obstacles, and I promise it will make you feel alive in every fibre. But my enthusiasm for climbing is running away with me. You see, I'm a believer in Scott—

> Sound, sound the clarion, fill the fife,
> To all the sensual world proclaim,
> One crowded hour of glorious life
>   Is worth an age without a name.

" Well, many thanks for your invitation : if my companions will allow me to desert them I will go with you gladly. Merely as a lover of Wordsworth I would like to see the Pillar."

" Yes, but don't come in a Wordsworthian frame of mind : if your brain is preoccupied with that 'something far more deeply interfused' you won't do your share of looking after the rope. But I see candle flickerings in some of the upper rooms, which means bed-time I suppose. I warn you by the way, that you won't find the clothes you sent to be dried, outside your door in the morning. You'll have to hunt for your stockings amongst some four dozen pairs hanging over the stair rail, and someone else is sure to have run off with your underclothing by mistake. It's one of the amusements of the place. Good night, and good luck on the morrow! "

Such is a specimen Eastertide day at Wastdale Head. For barely a week the overflowing Hotel resembles topsey-turveydom and the hills are dotted all over with irreverent pigmies. Then comes a sudden change. The climbers tramp off with knapsack and rücksack to Boot, Keswick, or Windermere, or drive to Seascale : once again the Hotel is left to hardy pedestrains and lovers of quietness, disturbed only by occasional coaches bringing people up from the coast for the day : once again the mountains resume their lonely spell; cragsmen will come at times but their manners will be more reserved. Tourists will appear at breakfast wearing cuffs and ties without exposing themselves to derision, and may even hire ponies and guides to Sca Fell Pike without being looked on contemptuously.

But the climber will find delight at Wastdale whether he go in or out of season, and will be puzzled to decide whether he enjoys most the wild seclusion of the place at the one time or the outlandish life and good fellowship at the other.

STACK GILL FIRST PITCH

III. STACK GILL.

"Haw! beginners, I presume," was the first remark
that caught our attention as a highly important little
man, with some genial companions, entered the hall
of the hotel.   Craig and I were lounging about the
porch of the " Fish " at Buttermere at the end of a
hot summer's day, and, the waggonette which
brought the newcomers having rumbled off, we were
settling down once more to enjoy the twilight and the
soothing chatter of Sail Beck, when our wandering
thoughts were arrested by the scornful insinuation.
Each of us glanced quickly at the other, and then
at the group inside : it was evidently our new rope
that had called forth the remark.   "Who are they?"
we wondered, and then, I think, consoled ourselves
with the reflection that we would shew them the next
day whether we were beginners or not.

An admission is hardly needed that practically we
were beginners;   our touchiness on the subject
betrays the fact, for an old mountaineer would have
been more amused than nettled at being thought a
novice on account of having a new rope with him.
We had only enjoyed the sport of rock-climbing for
a few years and our list of achievements would not
have been long, though we could have spent night
after night in recounting them, but we thought of

what we had discovered that day and would climb
the next, almost believing that we had already
vanquished a fine gully which had never yet been
tried even.   We had been exploring and photographing on the Haystacks, up and down gullies and
crags, but without finding anything that required
more than a short rope, until late in the afternoon,
when, having worked round the rocks overlooking
the lake and reached the great hollow of Warnscale
beyond, we discovered three clefts worthy of a place
on Gable.   The shadows creeping up Fleetwith,
and certain inner cravings, reminded us of the
" Fish," but we resolved that on the morrow our
new rope should do good service, and at dinner I
fancy that our enthusiasm afforded considerable
amusement to the Artist.   " You remind me," he
said, " of a man at one of the Scottish Mountaineering
Club dinners at Fort William describing a climb,
' Magnificent ! '—ay, that was it—' no foothold !
and scarcely any handhold ! and the rocks absolutely
perpendicular !—*absolutely perpendicular!!* '   Ha !
a grand climb—and now all the writers in the
Journal want to use the same expression, and the
Editor has to compress it into A.P. for want of
space," and the Artist chuckled as he repeated to
himself " ' No foothold, and scarcely any handhold !
Magnificent.' "

The following day we were out early, before the
newcomers were down.   The sun was already hot
and we left jackets and waistcoats behind and

walked with eagerness to Warnscale Bottom. Very few Lake District climbs are easier to reach—from the road a scramble of 500 feet up a grassy slope takes you half way to the base of the cliffs, and if the remaining 500 feet of steep scree prove toilsome, a desire to weigh up the difficulties in front will be ample excuse for a halt. From the scree slope the three gullies are well seen, fairly close together, and about half way between the Haystacks' top and Green Crag. The central fissure, insignificant below, terminates in a long, fine-looking chimney; from a distance both this and the left-hand cleft are seen to end a hundred feet below the sky line, the angle of the cliff gradually falling back towards the top. On approaching the rocks however, this gentler slope is hidden and the sky line appears bold and romantic. Rock-towers, as of an Italian hill-city, surround the top of the left-hand gully, and lower down in it a huge pillar, separated from the main cliff by a branch of the gully, is an imposing feature : the apparent stability of these fine square-cut blocks must be rather deceptive however, for Mr. Robinson tells me that one of the largest rock-falls remembered in the district took place here about 1886, and, indeed, the lower part of this left-hand Y gully is easily seen to be excessively rotten. Fine as they are, we hardly looked at these two gullies—it was the right-hand one that attracted all our attention, partly because of its finish, a chasm 20 or 30 feet wide, reaching to the cliff top, with hints of inner chimneys here and there, but chiefly on account of its base, a great wedge of mysterious darkness, suggesting all kinds of possibilities. When we came to close quarters the darkness resolved itself into a deep cleft between walls, smooth and unclimbable looking, from 6 to 10 feet apart; but the back of the gully appeared feasible enough, and when once we were over the boulder, 30 feet up, that made such a cavern at the foot of the cleft, no doubt we should get on famously.

We soon found that the back of the gully was not quite so dry as it looked from a distance. I climbed up a narrow inner chimney, and, standing on a jammed stone in a sort of shower bath, I could touch the boulder which roofed the cave and projected some distance beyond me. It seemed as though it would be easiest to climb higher up into the black hole and try if I could not get behind the boulder, but no opening was to be found and I had to return, rather wetter and dirtier, to the jammed stone. I next attempted to traverse out so as to get beyond the boulder. This was easy enough, but after getting clear of the boulder and clinging to the wall with one hand, I sought in vain for a handhold higher up, and soon had to return once more to the chimney. Craig then offered to take the lead : his reach is extraordinary—when heights and reaches were being marked on the wall at Wastdale he asked " Why on the wall? " and astonished everyone by making a streak on the ceiling—I felt sure that *he* would find a handhold. Yet after feeling about as I had done, but higher, and even getting his hand on the boulder, he found nothing to catch hold of, for, though rough and jagged below, it was perfectly rounded by the water above. One important fact he discovered, however—there was a small hole behind it through which the rope might be threaded. He quickly returned to the chimney, untied, pushed quantities of rope through the hole until the end dropped over in front, and then tied himself on and proceeded to try once more. With this safeguard he could afford to be much more venturesome, and after getting out of the chimney he managed with some trouble to assume a backing-up position across the gully; but with all his length it was too wide for him : his feet were level with his shoulders and he could not move upwards in the least. After this I took a turn again, and tried the effect of backing out under the boulder and holding on to its under surface. I managed to find a precarious ledge for one foot, rather higher than before, and was able to reach over the boulder to the hole through which the rope was threaded. My fingers groped round it for some providentially placed sharp crack or angle—alas, they only brought out a number of loose little stones, which rolled over, clicked at the bottom of the gully, and rattled away down the screes. Craig, who could not see the look on my face, thought I was doing well and shouted up encouragements—he gets drunk with delight on the

mountains and apostrophises rocks and torrents in
a way that would astonish anyone who knew him
only in town. " Ha ! ha ! we've had our 'Colenso'
and ' Magersfontein,' but it's your turn now old
gully ! your 'Paardeberg' has come to-day." " It
looks to me more like utter defeat," I replied,
" there's nothing for it but to descend again."
" Nay ! nay ! stick at it man, ' No turning back.'
You're in a fine position now and you can't fall."
No use—I came down, and we had lunch for a
variation. " 'Once more into the breach,' " said
Craig, when we had finished, and we climbed into
the cave with renewed determination. Again and
again we tried, but all to no purpose, and finally we
wandered home in a subdued frame of mind
(attuned to the still evening, let us say). It was not
our first failure or we might have felt it more. For
some time we visited Lakeland and succeeded with
almost everything we attempted (the probable
reason being that we only attempted things with
which we felt sure of success), but one luckless day,
on our way up the North Climb on the Pillar,
Savage Gully, the unclimbed, fascinated us, and
from that day onwards our shorter holidays seemed
to be wholly spent in returning to vain attacks on it.
Our present failure, therefore, was not so galling
as it might have been : we thought of the day's
delights—of the hot-looking blaze on Fleetwith,
seen from the cool recesses and framed by the dark
walls of our gully—of the stream's faint monotone

borne towards us from below at intervals—of the grip of the rough rock—but we couldn't quite banish the feeling that we had secretly meant to impress the newcomers at dinner, and as so often happens with people who mean to be impressive, we should end by appearing ridiculous as we deserved.

The Artist was at the door when we reached the hotel. " Well, have you scaled the ledgeless walls of the impending precipice? " he asked with a twinkle in his eye. " You ought to have done something prodigious ! I think you're more covered with clean dirt than any couple I've ever seen— sweeping the moss out of the chimney with your white flannels, eh? " We told of our defeat at which he laughed sympathetically, and enjoined us to make ourselves presentable quickly. At dinner the feelings we had entertained towards the new-comers were modified after hearing of their doings. They had only been the Easy way up the Pillar and the little man, whose remark had so irritated us, had not accompanied them. " The fact is, I wasn't quite well, I think—rather bilious in fact—and the look of the slab made me feel giddy, so I let the others go on without me."

" Perhaps just as well you didn't cross," said Craig wickedly, " you might have stuck at the top instead of the bottom. Why, man," he continued, turning to me, " we might have had a repetition of last New Year's Eve."

" What happened then? " asked the Artist.

" We had an expedition to rescue a party that got crag-bound half-way up the Pillar : Opp' here was out of it, but my friend Shaw and I had a grand time in the snow and ice. I think I never had a more thrilling experience than when we got opposite the rock, at two or three in the morning, after struggling from Wastdale through the snow, in star and candle light, all the time not knowing where the poor chaps were, or whether they were dead or alive. We sent up a shout from the bottom of the valley, and then listened and looked upwards into the silence and darkness, and at last we saw a tiny light flicker for a moment high up on the rock. In all my life I never felt such a thrill as at that moment."

" Well, did you rescue the party ? "

" Nay, it was another failure ; the men were out all night, but they got off the rock before we reached them."

We spoke of failure with light hearts now that we knew something of the doings of our companions and their powers. Perhaps we might have returned to our earlier feelings of foolish self-satisfaction but for the presence of the Artist whose knowledge and experience kept us within bounds. How he laughed with us, after, at the remarks some cyclists had made. " I've heard them speak of bridge-inclines as hills before, but never until to-night, of A.P. mountain paths. I congratulate you on the way in which you restrained your smiles."

" Well, the time when we had most difficulty to

avoid laughing was when we heard of the little man's discomfiture on the Pillar; do you know, we thought from something we heard, that he must be a great climber, and we were a bit afraid of meeting him to-night after our fiasco.'

"Oh," said the Artist, "most beginners make fools of themselves in the same way. The most amusing example I remember was an American at Chamounix. He was sitting opposite me and next to a President of the Alpine Club, and started the conversation by announcing 'I have just returned from the ascent of The Mont Blanc.' 'Oh, indeed,' his neighbour replied. He continued, 'It is my opinion that The Mont Blanc is the most difficult mountain in Europe.' 'Ah,—do you think so?' The American got irritated that the stranger was so little impressed, and said, 'Have you, Sir, made the ascent of The Mont Blanc?' 'Oh, yes,—10 or 11 times—I forget which.' The poor fellow laid down his knife and fork and gazed at his neighbour and at last ejaculated 'My God! It's chronic!!' *He* didn't brag any more that night." We had a delightful evening with the Artist: he was a real mountain enthusiast, who knew almost every peak and glen in the Highlands, every valley in the Alps, and had racy tales connected with all of them. We thought ourselves thoroughly familiar with the Lake District, but though he didn't pretend to such an intimate acquaintance with it as with Scotland, he knew it better than we did. When he began to talk about the Highlands he was carried away with excitement : as he spoke of the boiling torrents of golden water rushing through the pines of Glen Affric, of the ranges of cliff on the Cairngorms, of Carn Eige and Scurr Ouran, his eyes dilated, and he would pause after the enjoyment of rolling out the Gaelic names, shake his head knowingly at us, and end up significantly with " My conscience."

Our holiday passed without further result, but we had the gully continually in mind, and Christmas week saw us once more tramping to Buttermere, this time with our friend Shaw, from whose prowess we hoped for success.   There was no snow on the Haystacks, but there had been plentiful rain, which made a sight for us at the foot of the gully.   Over the boulder a waterfall was pouring, and, as we fortified ourselves with bacon sandwiches, we looked up and already felt the cold stream down our necks. Craig had already become an adept at threading the rope and he offered to encounter the enemy first, if we would tie on and lead up.   He passed quickly where the water descended into the gully bed, and up the chimney behind it (half out of sight) where we hoped that he might be in comparative dryness. In a few minutes the rope appeared, and Craig pulled a long length through, that we might tie on in comfort.   He returned with every particle of clothing wet.   It was ridiculous to attempt the climb, but Craig had done his share and we had to do ours.   So, in turn, for ten minutes each, Shaw and I stuck to the wall with numb hands and feet. On emerging from below the boulder, a few seconds was time enough for the water to completely bathe us, and bubble out of the tops of our boots.   I fumbled about awhile, pretending to feel for hand-holds which I knew to be not there, and then, shivering, feeling as if my clothes weighed hundred-weights, and able to hold on no longer, I came down and let Shaw do likewise.   We took off a number of our garments and wrung them out, and had a race over the hills for the rest of the day to restore our feelings.

In spite of our experience we were at the foot of the gully once more the following morning; water was still pouring down it, though not so plentifully as on the day before, and we decided to try the climb by keeping to the right, and avoiding the boulder altogether.   Shaw took the lead, starting on the cliff 20 feet or more outside the Gully, and traversing upwards into it.   He made his way very cautiously up steep, rounded rocks, interspersed with heather, and tried to get into the chimney just above the boulder, but it proved impracticable. This was provoking, for above the boulder was a beautiful string of little chimneys and cracks of the kind which always appears to have been specially designed for climbers, with chock-stones at con-venient intervals for resting, and belaying pins for the rope where required, whereas the way up the gully in front of us, though not difficult, was rather risky. However, Shaw led very carefully, and 60 or 70 feet higher reached the back of the gully and the top of the first pitch. From immediately below no more can be seen than we had already climbed, but from here we could see to the top of the gully. The left wall is continuous, the right more or less broken away in this middle portion of the gully, but ending in a bold precipice on the sky line. A patch of scree was followed by 40 feet of back and knee work up a wet inner chimney, then more scree and and broken rocks, and then a rather awkward looking pitch formed by a wall of rock crossing the gully, through which the stream cuts in a corkscrew fashion. At the fourth pitch Shaw took to the rocks on the left wall, after which some easier scrambling led to the formidable last pitch, formed by steep rocks crossing from side to side, with a weak point on the right where they are broken by a cave 12 feet high, capped by a great boulder. This gave us considerable trouble. Shaw tried back-and-foot work, but the cave was too wide. The walls were too clean cut for climbing on, so he stood on Craig's shoulders, while I held the rope from the back of the cave. In this position he searched for some time for a handhold, and at last gave a spring, scraped up the top of the cave wall with his edge-nails and struggled out under the corner of the boulder. Craig scorned my shoulders and suc-ceeded with great difficulty in backing up. I was not tall enough for this and had to accept the aid of the rope. " Pull, Thomas, lad," I heard Craig say, and before I knew what was happening I was off my feet and appeared round the corner of the boulder, whence I struggled up as they had done, but amidst roars of laughter. " Well, we'll have champagne to-night after this," I said. " To christen the gully in, or as a thankoffering for your deliverance?" asked Shaw as we unroped. Craig was already free and had run up the 30 feet of scree which remained between us and the top of the ridge, where the glorious scene moved him to declaim variations on Wordsworth—

> " All hail, ye mountains! hail, thou evening light!
> Better to breathe at large on this clear height
> Than toil for gold in Manchester's foul gloom."

We quickly despatched the damp and broken remnants of our provisions, for the sun had set, and our old friend the Gable looked sleepily at us, withdrawing his snowy cap and white-lined cliffs into the mists of night.

" Now for a race to the Honister," said Craig, and off we set at a trot over the dark heather. The quick action was enjoyable after four and a half hours in the cold gully, and the view at the end superb. We came suddenly to the edge, and looked over into a mysterious purple gulf of darkness, intensified in colour and depth after glancing back at the fading daffodil twilight. We could have excused the cyclist if he had declared the tame screes of Dale Head opposite to be absolutely

perpendicular—they certainly looked quite unclimbable.   Darkness overtook us on the way down
Fleetwith, but before we reached Gatesgarth a faint
silver light wandered round the shoulders of High
Crag, and as we walked on to Buttermere, discussing
the gully's name, the moon shone brilliantly.
" Why not try to recall the old Norse name—High
Stacken, the high cliffs—' High Stack Gill,' how
would that do, eh? "   " Too grandiose."   " ' Stack
Gill ' then," and so it was settled.   We were happy
that night as we lay by the fire after dinner, and in
bed, hearing " snow-muffled winds " after Buttermere's two bells had duly celebrated the advent of
the 20th century, we congratulated ourselves that
we had not had snow and glazed rocks to contend
with amongst Stack Gill's difficulties.

For a while I thought no more about it but as
Easter drew near misgivings began to come; though
certainly not a failure, our climb had only been a
partial victory—we had avoided the most difficult
part, the cave at the foot.   The result of these
misgivings was that Craig and I once more returned
to the attack.   We tried 'scarpetti,' but again failed.
Then it struck me that I might push my ice-axe
through the hole behind the boulder and when high
enough use it as a handhold.   The device succeeded..   As before, I traversed out on the right
wall and up until I could see the point of the axe at
the back of the boulder.   Steadying myself with
one hand I was just able to grasp it with the other

and in another minute I was up. Above the boulder all was comparatively simple : the chimney narrowed, and led in a dozen feet to the second obstacle, a small group of jammed stones with an opening behind through which water fell from above. As the stones seemed doubtful to trust to I worked up behind them, filling up the hole in doing so and causing the water to change its course to my clothes and skin. Above this a narrowing series of short chimneys led to the junction with our former route.

The second direct ascent was made three months later by Mr. P. S. Thompson with his brother, and they thought the gully a very sporting one—equal in interest to Moss Gill, if nothing is shirked. They managed the first pitch by passing the rope through behind the boulder and using it as a handhold instead of an axe.

As this was our first new climb, we took a keen interest in it, and were a little disappointed not to hear of it being oftener visited, but one day last Easter I had the pleasure of seeing it fairly blocked with traffic. Seven of us were tramping up Warnscale towards another climb, when Haskett-Smith, who had climbed Stack Gill the year before, asked how many of the others had done it, and insisted on the whole party going there. This alone would have crowded the gully, but when we reached it we were surprised to find two other men struggling at the first pitch, so the climb may now be developing into a popular one. I hope it may give as many delightful days to others as it has given to us.

BOWFELL BUTTRESS

IV. BOW FELL BUTTRESS.

I ALWAYS look back with particular pleasure on a
certain June morning when I first met my two oldest
climbing comrades, Tom Shaw, and his friend
Craig.   They came upon me painting away at a
cloud effect on Bow Fell in a downpour of rain,
and, I suppose out of pity for my drenched
condition, invited me to join them in a scramble
which would warm me up. I resisted the temptation
and kept at my canvas, but in the evening we met
again in the Dungeon Gill smoke room and talked
about mountains and climbing until we almost felt
that we had known one another for ages.

My friends were enthusiastic novices, and were
highly elated at having discovered, in the course of
their day's ramble, a fine new climb, as they thought,
on Bow Fell. I had been a novice a year or two
earlier and could therefore talk down to them from
the heights of great experience, so I laughed at the
idea of any really good climbing being found there,
particularly on the side facing Langdale, in full
view of the track. The district had been thoroughly
explored by first-rate men and they had probably
been deceived by the mist which had magnified
some minor crag into the huge pillar-like buttress
of their report. However they declared there was

no mistake—the pillar was undoubtedly large, and so steep on the face that they feared it could not be climbed on that side.

Often after that, when we were making holiday plans, a visit to Bow Fell Buttress was put down on the list, but it was always displaced by something which appeared at the moment more attractive, so that many years elapsed before we went near it, and then more by chance than premeditated choice. Five of us, staying at the snug little farm of Fell Foot, in Little Langdale, had arranged for a long expedition, but the morning outlook being bad, and the previous day on Doe Crags having been a hard one, we decided to stroll lazily to the Bow Fell Buttress and see whether there was any climb on it worth doing.

Three hours later we sat lunching on a rocky mound opposite the cliff, and I had to apologize for disparaging insinuations uttered so long before that I had almost forgotten them. All disagreement about the crag's worthiness was at an end, but a new one was begun about its height. While we lingered over dessert one of the party was observed to throw himself into mysterious attitudes reminiscent of the Louvre fighting gladiator, though the heroic and defiant effect was somewhat marred by the shutting of one eye and by a harmless pencil held in the uplifted hand in place of a "warlike shield." As a result of these contortions he informed us, after jotting down a little sum, that the height was 180 feet. For the credit of the rest of us I must add that no one believed him. The general verdict was 250 feet, but it proved to be half as high again.

Before walking across to the foot of the cliff we held a consultation about the route. The Buttress stood out commandingly from a wide hollow of screes on the left and was cut off from broken rocks on the right by a gully which wound round to its back, so that the further from the centre we started the shorter the climb would be, but the finest climb was evidently straight up the middle of it. We decided on some slightly marked cracks and chimneys running up the face of the Buttress,—not continuous, but we could see traverses that might join them, and it gave us pleasure afterwards to think that though our estimates of height proved absurdly wrong, we chose our way well, and followed it to within a few yards throughout.

It was quickly settled that the discoverers should have the posts of honour and Shaw started off, with Craig to back him up where necessary; then came West and Hargreaves and I brought up the rear. We started at the lowest point of the Buttress and scrambled to the foot of a chimney which made a long vertical line up the centre of the cliff. We intended to utilize this but found the lowest part of it overhanging in a very uncompromising way, so our leader took to a short chimney to the right of it, up which we all wriggled after him and reached a grassy terrace which led off the cliff to the right. It was suggested that we might have reached the same point by going round the cliff some way and walking up the terrace. This was undeniable, but then of course we might also have walked up the screes to the top of the Buttress if we had wished. It was the struggle to attain, not the attainment of the goal that we had come for. Above the terrace the cliff rose steeply, and though the excellent quality of the rock made very small ledges and knobs sufficient for foot and hand hold, the situation was exposed, and Shaw worked back to the left as soon as possible to get into the long chimney, which we had found unfeasible at the bottom. He passed out of sight now, and the next time I saw him he was with Craig, looking down from another grass terrace, ninety feet above me. The chimney offered no special difficulties; we admired, in passing, the design of a little sentry-box in the middle of it, and were soon all together again on the second terrace.

The chimney ended here, but we had noticed from our lunching place that by traversing to the right a little we might find our way upwards by an ill-defined gully. Our leader looked at the entrance to it, and did not like it. It seemed preferable to come back a yard or two and take to a vertical crack which led into the gully higher up. This seemed a good test of power of grip and firmness of climbing nails, and above the crack the rocks appeared by no means easy. Half an hour passed before my turn came to try, and I watched the heavy clouds hovering over the valley drop lower and lower until an arch was formed which rose from the gloom of Mickleden and swept across the Band into Oxendale—a vast cathedral portal, flanked by solemn walls of cold grey stone, and beyond, outside it, as one so often sees from a cathedral doorway, a blaze of light—the enamelled fields of Langdale glistening, emerald-like, and the Blea Tarn road, dusty in the sunshine, fluttering like a pale ribbon from the tip of the cloud arch down the hillside.

Most of the party were now out of sight, but I could hear words of warning or advice alternating with scratchings of the rock high up and uneasy enquiries as to progress lower down. At last I caught a glimpse of Shaw traversing round a perilous corner far above; after which the cloud dropped a little and I saw no more of him until we met on the summit. I began to suspect our estimates of the rock's height : measured by our rope the grass terrace where I was waiting was 140 feet from the base, and now word came down that our 160 feet of rope was all out and the leader still not near the top.

I found the crack easier than I had anticipated, but when I reached the traverse I felt doubtful whether I should have liked to lead there, for the handholds were poor, and, looking down, the base of the cliff seemed almost vertically beneath, though of course it was not really anything like so steep. Twenty feet higher the man above was waiting to stand on my shoulders. The next ledge was only 10 feet above him, but 10 feet was beyond even Craig's reach, and there was no lower handhold. When my turn came I took a jump up and the rope was pulled in until I could grip something. From this ledge a chimney 80 feet high led to the summit of the Low Man, where we built a cairn in the orthodox manner and congratulated Shaw and Craig on having discovered and mastered a first-rate new climb. Then we scrambled to the true summit of the Buttress, 30 feet higher and hurried back for dinner two hours overdue.

It was suggested that the next day we should retire to some comfortable knoll and lick our wounds; so we basked lazily in the sun listening to the call of the cuckoo down below amongst the blackthorn hedges and up above Blea Tarn. We strolled across to Dungeon Gill for tea, and made a careful distant survey of the Buttress, from which we found the height to be 370 feet. We also noted down the details of our climb in the book, but could in no way agree over one miserable little point, about which West reminded us.

" Don't forget to mention the 'sentry-box': the most comfortable spot on the cliff. I felt really happy there."

" From your looks no one would guess that you ever felt anything else," one replied, for he is always like a beam of sunshine amongst us, with a face ever radiant with contentment and goodwill.

" Ah, I have to dissemble to give you rash boys confidence ! But what a perfect little haven it was. A flat stone to stand on, your body most kindly embraced by the rocks and comfortable elbow rests at the right height. I just closed my eyes for two seconds and thought of dinner and cider, after a hot bath, and it was heavenly."

" Well, how will this do—'In the long chimney there is a little sentry-box which makes a good resting-place——' "

" Yes, that's all right."

" ' Midway between the two terraces——' "

" No," from four people at once.

" Why it's high above the second terrace," from one of them.

" Yes, of course ; in the gully above the crack," from another.

" But that isn't the long chimney : you can't call it a chimney at all."

" Well, that's what we thought you meant. It's just below the large belaying-pin."

" Above," from three others.

" But," I said, " I'm quite positive it's not in the gully at all. I remember looking up from the ' sentry-box ' and seeing you on the terrace beside the crack."

" The conceit of the man !" retorted Craig. " I suppose he thinks that because he has painted the mountain he knows the whole bag of tricks ! The impudence ! Next thing I expect he'll be whitewashing a country church and posing as a theologian on the strength of it."

We backed up our assertions with all sorts of circumstantial evidence, but argued in vain, and it became clear that we would have to pay another visit to settle the point, so at six the next morning, after watching the others drive off, homeward-bound, Craig and I set our faces again in the direction of Bow Fell.

Our early start gave us the sight for the first time of a Lakeland fox-hunt. As we walked up Rossett Gill the whole hollow resounded with the yelping and baying of dogs, and we were surprised at the time we took to locate the noise. A couple of buzzards circling round and round near the Buttress attracted our attention. "Ha," said Craig, "the word has gone forth that there shall be no more solitude on their old nesting-place. I wonder whether they have been boding ill since our climb." But it was something else that made them hover there, for immediately below were the hounds, distinct enough now we had spotted them, but looking no more impressive than a lot of wretched little maggots aimlessly wriggling over the rough ground, in and out of hollows, up and down the rocks, incessantly moving, without making much progress, so that we got almost up to them as they passed the foot of our climb and made away round Flat Crags. West wrote to me that he knew from the twinkles in our eyes that we would not go to the rock's base without climbing it again, and we certainly roped and started up without attempting to settle the disputed point from below. It was not long before the one was found to be right and the four wrong, but we had a good excuse for continuing, for we had taken an aneroid with us and thought we would check our survey. For the first few pitches all went well: I made a note of our height in the "sentry-box" and then climbed up the long chimney while Craig paid out 40 feet more rope. At the top of the chimney the aneroid indicated a rise of only 10 feet. This was discouraging, but I thought I might have made a mistake. We got together again on the upper terrace, and then I climbed the crack and right on until our 80 feet rope ran out. I took the barometer out once more and it again showed a rise of only 10 feet. Craig came up and we looked at the aneroid together in silence until, while we watched it, the finger went slowly back to 10 feet below the terrace we started from: then we relieved our pent-up feelings and pocketed the fickle instrument.

The next part of the climb was the piece that, on the first ascent, seemed to me the most dangerous, but at the start there is a grand belaying-pin and from this Craig paid out the rope until I reached the square corner. It really felt much easier this time to lead up than before to follow—a thing I have frequently noticed with climbs well within my powers, and can only account for by supposing the nervous strain of watching others struggling up in front to more than counterbalance the confidence inspired by having a rope above and a good man to hold it.

Craig now came up, and, suggesting that the corner might be turned by a détour instead of making a direct attack on it, he led the way, effecting a great improvement in the climb by rendering a shoulder up unnecessary.

Throughout both ascents the last man had removed all the loose stones he could find, but this time I distinguished myself by unintentionally sending down from the final chimney a block of two or three hundredweights, which we had all in turn used in climbing. I was backing up with my feet against it when it slowly heaved over, gave one bound against the rock and then flew right out into a gulf of sunlit cloud and rainbow below us and was lost to sight. Some seconds of silence, and then a tremendous crash far down, followed by a fusillade of fragments and the prolonged baying of the startled fox-hounds on the opposite side of Flat Crags. It was lucky that I had just given up the lead and that there was no one in the chimney below.

As almost invariably happens the second ascent robbed Bow Fell Buttress of some of the difficulties with which our imaginations had invested it, but we still consider it a most interesting climb, furnishing grandly exposed situations, and cannot understand why a cliff so discernable from a frequented path has been so long overlooked. It may be that its position on Bow Fell dwarfs its appearance. Most of our Lakeland cliffs are hidden away and only properly seen from some high hollow where the size of the mountains they are on cannot be grasped at the same time, and compared with them. Pavey Ark cliffs, for instance, are 400 feet high, but their impressiveness is only seen from Stickle Tarn, barely 300 feet below them; Doe Crags occupy over half the height from Goat's Water to the summit, and Great End cliffs almost as much from Sprinkling Tarn, while the Sca Fell precipice owes something of its supremacy in grandeur to the fact that it cannot be well seen without climbing to Hollow Stones. Now Bow Fell's full height is seen along with the Buttress, and the latter, being only a seventh of the whole, is dwarfed into insignificance. Still, this explanation is not a satisfactory one, for the Napes on Great Gable are in just the same position, less in height, and yet look magnificent, and attract climbers as much as any rocks in England. But we are very exclusive in our choice of playgrounds. On Sca Fell, the Pillar and the Gable, we know that we are amongst the aristocracy of climbs, and most of us would rather make a single new ascent there than half a dozen on any other English crags, but their exploration has been so thorough that little has been left for us, and most of us in search of pioneer work have to be content with cliffs of no repute, which nevertheless will often yield as good a day's sport as the far-famed ones near Wastdale.

THE GREAT PITCH, FLEETWITH GULLY.

V. BUTTERMERE AS A CLIMBING CENTRE.

When tourists begin to make their way on ponies to the foot of Sca Fell crags; when a cobbler finds it profitable to open a hut at Row Head where thin tan shoes may be decorated with edge-nails; when every second person one meets there carries a rope and ice-axe in order to be correctly attired for the district—then perhaps climbers may begin to talk of Wastdale as many do now about Zermatt—as a place to be avoided by all mountaineers who think more of the sport than of doing famous climbs. And yet men of the old school, who love to tell of the delights of unknown centres, still furtively visit Zermatt and put up with its luxuries for the sake of seeing once more the grandest ring of mountains in the Alps. Though they talk deploringly of the poor Matterhorn bound with ropes and chains they know full well that it looks still as glorious as in the days when Ruskin and Whymper wrote of it, and that there are still ways up it where they are unlikely to be either jostled by other parties or insulted by artificial aids.

And so also with Wastdale Head: the rock-climber is unlikely to find any centre in Lakeland to vie with it even when the much-dreaded desecration comes. It has the three finest climbing grounds

—Sca Fell, Gable and Pillar—all close at hand, and others, such as Great End and the Screes within quite convenient distance. But most of us like a change at times, though it may not always be for the better. As secondary centres, Rosthwaite, Coniston, Great Langdale, Eskdale and Buttermere are all very delightful, and although no one of them offers the same variety of climbing as Wastdale, they all have compensations in the greater softness and richness of their valley scenery.

It is, however, only of Buttermere that I want to write, for I feel that, compared with Rosthwaite, Langdale and Coniston, it has in the past been unduly neglected by climbers. For beauty of wood and water it is equal to any of these centres. It has most comfortable hotels, and for those who prefer a farmhouse nearer the climbs there is Gatesgarth at the head of the lake, standing in the same relation to Buttermere as a centre that Seathwaite does to Rosthwaite, Stool End to Dungeon Gill, Butterilkel to Boot and Torver to Coniston. Few climbers seem to know how easily the Ennerdale cliffs on Gable can be reached from Buttermere, or that it is quite as good a base as Wastdale, if not better, for all the finest climbs on the Pillar—those on the north and west sides—while fewer still have any idea of the number of fine gullies close at hand. The following list of climbs within easy reach shows how well Buttermere compares with its more popular rivals :—

BUTTERMERE.	ROSTHWAITE.	LANGDALE.	CONISTON.
Walker's Gully.			
Pillar North-West Climb.			
	Eagle's Nest Ridge.		
	Sergeant Crag Gully.		
			Easter Gully.
	Kern Knotts Crack.		
			Doe Crag, Central Chimney.
Haskett Gully.			
Warn Gill.			
Birkness Chimney.			
Toreador Gully.			
		Gimmer Crag, *A route.*	
			Intermediate Gully.
		Gimmer Crag, *B route.*	
	Kern Knotts, West Chimney.		
Shamrock Chimney.			
Shamrock Gully.			
West Jordan Gully.			
Fleetwith Gully (direct).			
Pillar West Wall Climb.			
Stack Gill.			
	Raven Crag Gully.		
			Doe Crag, North Gully.
			Doe Crag Buttresses.
		Bow Fell Buttress.	
Pillar North Climb.			
	Mouse Gill.		
	Ling Chimney.		
		Crescent and Gwynne's Chimney.	
		Rake End Chimney.	
Bleaberry Chimney.			
			Doe Crag, Great Gully.

List of Climbs—*Continued.*

BUTTERMERE.	ROSTHWAITE.	LANGDALE.	CONISTON.
	Arrowhead.		
	Napes Needle		
High Stile Central Gully.			
		Gimmer Crag Chimney.	
Oblique Chimney.	Oblique Chimney.		
	Kern Knotts Chimney.		
Gable Crag, Central Gully.	Gable Crag, Central Gully.		
Doctor's Chimney.	Doctor's Chimney.		
High Stile, Black Chimney.			
	Great End, Central Gully.	Great End, Central Gully.	
Birkness Gully.			
Fleetwith Gully (easy way).			
Robinson's Green Crag Gully.			
		Pavey Ark Gullies.	
Yew Crag Gully.			
	Needle Ridge.		
Grasmoor Gullies.			
	Walla Crag Gully.		
	Combe Gill.		
Bottle-shaped Pinnacle Ridge.	Bottle-shaped Pinnacle Ridge.		
Pillar, West Climb.			
	Great End, South-east Gully.	Great End, South-east Gully.	

_____

(These climbs are roughly arranged in order of difficulty, beginning with the most severe).

It may be objected that "within easy reach" is extremely vague. To men like the holder of the Lakeland Fell record any climb in the district would probably be considered within easy reach from any spot in Lakeland. I myself have several times had climbs on Gable, Sca Fell and Pillar from Keswick, but it must be admitted that those days were taken up chiefly with the ramble to and from the crags. Some men may want to reckon the Pillar amongst Rosthwaite climbing grounds, but if the Rosthwaite list were extended in this way, the Buttermere list would also have to be enlarged to include Sergeant Crag and the south side of Gable, so that little difference would be made in the relations of the lists to one another. But it is more particularly to the possibilities of the valley itself that I want to draw attention. I have spent many holidays there, some with one or two of our best rock-climbers, some with men of my own more moderate powers, others with my wife and children, and have never yet been at a loss to find expeditions both new and suitable for all capacities. My wife and children have delightful memories of rambles through the pine woods; of boating on Crummock Water; of bilberry gathering high up on the rib of Fleetwith, and racing down its narrow grassy angle, with miles of the valley spread out beneath; of butterfly-collecting along the river, edged with meadow-sweet, between the two lakes; of bathing in the lovely pools hidden away in Warnscale. Angling hardly requires mention, for Buttermere is perhaps better known to the followers of Isaac Walton than to any other class of men. But there are plenty of opportunities for more arduous sport. I have described at some length, in an earlier chapter, the struggles we had to accomplish our first good climb in this district— Stack Gill. There are many others worth doing on the Haystacks. At the Scarth Gap end there are several easy chimneys suitable for beginners, and there is a rake, running up the cliff from near the foot of the big stack to the top of Stack Gill, after the manner of Jack's rake on Pavey Ark.

Let us make a tour of the valley, from right to left, and notice the various climbs as we pass them.

Beginning at Stack Gill, which has already been described, we come in about 100 yards to Warn Gill, a very difficult gully, the first ascent of which was made on May 24th, 1907, by Messrs. Fred Botterill, Adam Fox, J. R. Scott, T. Shaw and myself. We had a party of twenty at Buttermere that Whitweek, and as it included a couple of novices and some ladies, of whom two had done very little rock-climbing before, we had several easy days, and had to provide, as a compensation, a few stiff things on which ardent spirits like Botterill might work off their stored-up energy. Amongst these were Warn Gill and a gully on High Crag which proved rather more than difficult enough.

The start of the climb is not at all imposing. It is a narrow vertical chimney 25 or 30 feet high, very innocent-looking, cutting through a rock which is thrust out so as to allow of only a glimpse of the deep gully behind, higher up. At the top of this chimney—level with a broad platform —is a chockstone over which poured a small stream of water, not conspicuous, but we noticed that Botterill, in leading up, kept as far out of the chimney as he could, to avoid it, and did not pause at the chockstone, which is a little awkward to get over through being smooth and waterworn. Above the sloping platform comes an easy 10 ft. pitch, and then the gully begins to lead deeply into the cliff. The third pitch is about 25 feet, and can be climbed without much difficulty on the right wall. At the top of it a whiff from the remains of a sheep, which must have fallen down the gully, stimulated us to hurry to the foot of the most imposing pitch in the climb—a black cleft 70 or 80 feet high, down which water falls plentifully, and beating against a rock, is deflected, or rather appears to spring with a knowing malice on to any spot where the climber thinks he will be safe from it. The first 40 feet can be chimneyed, through the spray. Then the right wall falls back and it becomes necessary to climb to a sloping ledge on it. Botterill was perched on this for a long while, considering what ought to be the next move. He found a lizard running about over the vertical rocks and would have been glad if he could have ascended the next 15 feet in a similar manner. Looked at from below a good row of

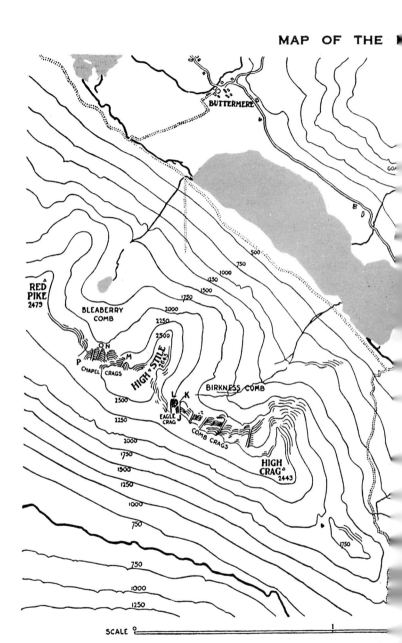

SCALE

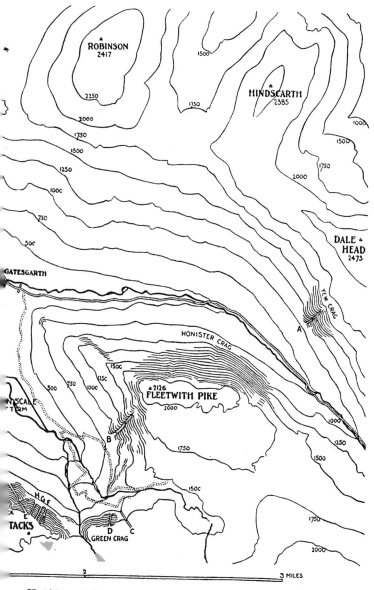

holds a little above him seemed to form a hand traverse leading back to the top chockstone, but from where he was he could see that they were on big blocks resting very insecurely on a ledge, and ready at a pull to part company with the wall behind them and sweep us all out of the gully. He came to the conclusion that he would need a shoulder, and, descending to us for a rest, asked me to go up and see what assistance I could give him. I found that everything looked much worse than from below, and after some consideration I recommended Shaw as a safer man for the post, and came down again fairly drenched. Shaw, having got on to the sloping ledge, thought he could manage. Botterill followed him and climbed on to his shoulders, whence, by a very difficult upward traverse to the left, he avoided the row of almost overhanging loose blocks, and got above the chockstone. He was still not in a good place for belaying, and went 80 feet higher, up mossy rocks which were steep but not difficult, to reach good anchorage. Shaw then followed and stayed at the top of the chockstone to direct and assist the rest of us. I came next, and found the piece above the ledge very trying even with a good deal of help from the rope. The loose blocks were just where I wanted to go, but they had to be carefully avoided. Having got up I passed Shaw and relieved Botterill at the belay, while he took stock of what was to follow. The next man happened to touch one of the blocks and over it

went, crashing down the gully. Luckily Scott was
in a sheltered corner. Being the last, he had the
enjoyment of hurling down the sources of danger,
and discovered in their place a few holds which may
make a difference to future parties.

We were now 250 feet up, and able to see the
finish, 150 feet or more above us. The greater part
of it went well enough. Two or three chimneys in
quick succession led to the final pitch, in the left-
hand corner of the gully, which from lower down
had had by no means an unyielding look, but the
higher we got the steeper it seemed, and now we
were up to it we found something like the corner
of a room—a very rottenly-built corner too—30 or
40 feet high and overhanging at the top. No one
suggested trying it. Botterill traversed 20 feet to
the right and attempted to get up the rock wall
there. This also failed. Shaw and Scott were on
another rope 50 feet below us, and Botterill asked
them to make for the foot of a grassy chimney which
led out at the right-hand corner of the gully. They
reported that it might go, and he descended to join
them. He then climbed half-way up the grassy
chimney, and if fine weather had continued might
have succeeded, but a thunderstorm suddenly burst
over us, and though we had all been sufficiently
soaked in the difficult pitch below to be careless of
the rain, the torrents which came down made the
chimney unsafe. Botterill asked Shaw and Scott to
go down again, and try still farther to the right, and

we followed them up a very steep rib of rock and heather, ending at the cliff top in a small chimney which should be pleasant enough in normal weather, but which was just then like a funnel down which a waterspout was being poured, and through this we had to pass to reach the summit. "Warnscale Gill" was suggested for the gully's name, but was cut down by the majority to "Warn Gill."

A hundred yards further to the left—nearest to Green Crag of the trio—is the Y gully. Messrs. J. W. Robson, Adam Fox, P. Spencer and I tried this in 1902. We got up 150 feet, and were not stopped by any special difficulty, but found the rock so rotten that we decided to go no further, and were glad enough to get safely down again. Higher up there appeared to be very fine pitches in both branches, but we thought it too risky to try and reach them.

Passing a beautiful little stream which tosses down a ravine from a small tarn on the moor above, we come to Green Crag. On the crag proper there is a very fine rift which Haskett-Smith christened the Toreador Gully from a pleasant incident at the top after he, Scott-Tucker and I had been exploring it. We attacked it under the impression that it was the Green Crag Gully, first climbed by Messrs. J. W. Robinson and W. A. Wilson in 1889. Robinson once told me that it was his bad description of the first ascent of Moss Gill which led to the second ascent being made by the splendid Collier finish, and, in the present case, his note that the climb was up the centre of Green Crag, set us on to something very much finer. We got half-way up the gully, and reached a place where a large loose block lay, covering a ledge which it was essential for us to use as a foothold. Tucker was under cover, much lower down, but Haskett-Smith could not move out of the line of fire, so we retreated, and descended the gully from the crag top, until we came to the loose block, which slid off, and mercilessly raked the chimney below, at the first touch. Nothing more was accomplished that day, but on August 2nd, 1908, Messrs. H. B. Lyon, E. H. P. Scantlebury, A. R. Thomson and I made the first ascent. The beginning is short but stiff and a shoulder is useful. After a long easy stretch the great pitch is reached. It is a wet chimney about 80 feet high, getting more and more severe up to the very top. It can be climbed with the back on the left wall and feet on the right, until the end is close at hand, when it becomes necessary to make a most awkward twist round in order to use the ledges on the left wall. There are no belays in the upper part of the chimney, but the second man can brace himself firmly across it, close under the leader, to stop him in case of a slip at this critical point. Above this there are only two easy pitches.

Robinson's Green Crag Gully is well to the left of the Toreador Gully, and is really off the crag altogether. It looks an imposing black cleft from

Buttermere, but is rather an impostor.   It is best climbed on a fairly dry day, for a stream comes down it, and, after heavy rain, the 70 ft. pitch, which presents the first difficulty, may be quite impossible. Even in normal weather a party which keeps conscientiously to the back of the gully is likely to reach the summit fairly soaked.

Further still to the left, in the centre of the face of Fleetwith, which looks towards the Haystacks, there is a prominent gully.   As a whole it is not at all steep or difficult, but it contains two very fine pitches which are both.   The first ascent was made by Messrs. G. T. Ewen, P. S. Minor, E. Broxap and D. Thompson, who, however, avoided these two pitches.   The following year, two other Rücksack Club men, Messrs. Laurence P. Scott and P. Ryan, made the first direct ascent.   Both of the difficult pitches are very interesting to climb, but the upper of the two is, in addition, really noble to look at— one of the most imposing in Lakeland.   Like all the best Buttermere pitches, they are liable to be very wet.

The other face of Fleetwith, between Gatesgarth and the Honister, has plenty of opportunities for rather indefinite scrambling, but on Honister Crag itself, where fine climbing might have been found, quarrying has made it impracticable.

On Dale Head, opposite, there is a gully in the centre of Yew Crag, first climbed on Good Friday, 1908, by Messrs. J. R. Scott, J. W. Robson,

A. Fox, G. R. West, Zimmern and myself. It is well seen from the Honister road about a mile and a third above Gatesgarth. The first big pitch is extremely difficult—perhaps impossible, though it is rash to say this of any climb. Scott and I tried it for some time, but could not get more than two-thirds way up, and we finally gave in and climbed round it on the left wall. Other men may get some good sport in trying the pitch direct, but apart from this the gully is just a pleasant easy scramble.

If we continue our tour round the valley the next definite climbs we come to are two long easy gullies on the north-west side of Grasmoor, facing the foot of Crummock Water. These are capital climbs for beginners. The one nearest Buttermere gives most sport. It is easily reached by following the Cockermouth road for a mile and a half and then striking straight up the grassy slopes to the foot of it. Most of the awkward places in it can be avoided if the novice finds them too difficult, but he will discover many interesting little problems if he adheres strictly to the back of the gully. Its very considerable length is a point in its favour, and the view from the top is one of the finest in the district.

Crossing the valley, we come to some much more difficult though shorter gullies in Bleaberry Combe, on the side of High Stile. When looking up at the chief crag, from near the tarn, a long narrow chimney will be seen between the Central Gully and the scree shoot to the right of the cliff. This was first ascended on Easter Monday, 1908, by Messrs. W. P. Haskett-Smith, Eric Greenwood, W. A. Brigg, H. Scott-Tucker and myself, and is the longest and most enjoyable climb on these crags. To the left of it is the Central Gully, a not very continuous climb, with two stiff pitches, and still further to the left, hardly visible from the tarn, though well seen from the Buttermere Hotel, is the Black Chimney, a short climb of two pitches, the second of which offers a good struggle. Both these climbs were made by Messrs. O. G. Jones and J. W. Robinson in 1893.

In the centre of the next hollow—Birkness Combe —stands Eagle Crag, the finest rock in the Buttermere valley. It has a flat top, somewhat below the ridge of the amphitheatre, from whose sloping sides it projects, and two main surfaces, at right angles to each other, one facing the head and the other the foot of the Lake. At the angle, where it stands out most, the height is about 350 feet. The most formidable-looking climb on it is a very straight gully close to the angle, where the crag is steepest. The face which looks towards Gatesgarth is separated from the more broken-up crag to the left of it, by an overhanging gully less than half the height of the first. Between these two gullies there is a 240 ft. chimney which almost meets the Straight Gully at the top, behind a tower of rock at the angle. Dr. Sheldon and I had a good look at these climbs in 1903. The chimney, though perhaps not the most difficult, seemed the most interesting of the three,

and we tried it first.   The first pitch was merely a
grassy angle; then came a 20 ft. wet rock chimney,
followed by another, rather wetter one, of 30 feet.
There was no avoiding the water here, for the lower
part had to be backed up against a streaming wall,
and in the upper part we had to apply ourselves to,
and pull over, an equally streaming slab, while a
shower-bath descended on us from a rock above.
From this pitch we emerged, dripping, on to a grassy
terrace which can be reached without climbing the
chimney, by an easy scramble alternately to right and
left of it.   There is always something disappointing
about a pitch which can be avoided : even Moss Gill
(in most ways an ideal climb) would be improved if
there were no chance of evading the first two pitches
and the direct finish.   Above the terrace we found a
wall of rock facing us, with a 25 ft. chimney on its
left.   Sheldon chose the latter; I preferred the wall,
which, though vertical, had capital pockets for hand
and foot.   At the top there was just standing room
for the two of us, and the next pitch—a stiff little
crack—followed immediately.

Above this the chimney widens out, and luckily
the bed of it is not quite so steep, or we should have
had little chance of success, for the sixth pitch is the
great difficulty of the climb, and it was necessary for
me to be well placed close to the leader in case of a
slip.   The chimney runs up into a cave formed by a
large overhanging mass of rock which is thrust out
from the left wall, and makes progression on that

side impossible. High above our heads, on the right side, it left an almost vertical shallow groove, and the problem before us was how to reach this. We could find no belay, so I jammed myself as tightly as possible at the top of the cave, while Sheldon worked outwards to clear the overhanging rocks. He used both sides of the chimney as far as possible; then the stretch became too great, and the only thing to be done was to push off from the left wall and make a spring for what seemed a handhold higher up on the right. Was it a handhold, however? That was an important point, for the foothold on the right wall was only good enough to trust to for a second while making the spring, and if the apparent handhold turned out to be a sloping ledge Sheldon would probably shoot down the chimney and I was hardly jammed tightly enough to withstand a pull of this kind. We decided that it was too risky without first seeing it from above, and we descended and went round to the top of the chimney. We got down it far enough to see that the handhold was good, but we found that danger was not over after getting into the groove we wished to reach, and we had to consider whether the climb was justifiable without a good belay.

There is great diversity of opinion as to what renders a climb unjustifiable. I myself hold that neither extreme difficulty, nor extreme danger in case of a slip, are sufficient by themselves to relegate a climb to this class. The most difficult problem that

I have seen is the top pitch of Walker's Gully, but though the climb is on an overhanging wall, with a tremendous drop below it, if the rope is properly threaded and looked after, there is nothing to fear. Then as to the danger in case of a slip. There are many places—some on quite easy climbs—where, if the leader fell, the second man would have very little chance of saving him, owing to scarcity of belays. But in most of these places a climber would be no more likely to fall than would the average man from, say, a path along the edge of a cliff—where a slip would be equally dangerous. But as soon as the leader feels that the climb is in any way taxing his powers in a place devoid of anchorage, to go on is to allow discretion to give way to daring.

In this case we concluded that we must find a good belay or give up the climb. We had an idea that an ice-axe might be placed behind some projecting rocks in such a way as to serve the purpose, and took one up on our next visit. It had been the occasion of some chaffing down below (being August), it was a nuisance on the way up, and when we had got it we could not fix it firmly enough. However, I used the pick to root out all the moss and loose stuff from a small crack at the back of the cave, and at length found a stone firmly jammed in it. Behind this, after a number of fruitless attempts, we succeeded in threading the rope, after which I could hold it from Sheldon's level lower down and could give him some assistance until he got his upper half into the groove. It was comical to watch his feet dangling below the overhanging block, making an occasional futile effort to scrape up on the wall, and very slowly disappearing. After some minutes he gained a standing place and hauled up the ice-axe and coats, weighty with water again, for the chimney was, if anything, wetter than when we first tried it. I followed with great difficulty, especially after getting my shoulders into the groove which was covered with green slime, and had to be ascended by a most uncomfortable kind of chimneying—elbow and hand. When once the foot was high enough for edge nails to grip in the groove it was simpler, and a good pull over a chockstone at the top completed the sixth pitch. The seventh was another of 20 feet up a broken vertical wall at the back of the chimney; the eighth and last was quite easy and took us to a wall built across the top of the chimney to prevent sheep from getting near it.

While we were at the top it seemed worth while preparing the way for an attempt on the short gully into which the east face of Eagle Crag runs. From below it has very much the aspect of Walker's Gully on a very small scale, and is similarly surmounted by a funnel-shaped scree-shoot, which pours any superfluities over the topmost boulder. We sent down some hundredweights of loose stones, which were perilously near going without our aid, but left the climb for another day.

The lower part is very easy. A mossy cave is

soon reached, and from this we worked straight up for some distance, passing at the back of some tempting stones which were rather doubtfully jammed and which we refrained from using. The pitches were very indefinite until we reached a large cave within 12 or 15 feet from the under side of the crowning boulder. On a level with this cave, but some distance out, is another huge boulder which bridges across the gully. The best method of procedure is for the leader to stay in the cave while the second man traverses out on to the bridge, from which he can climb up into a higher cave, immediately under the top boulder, and thread the rope there. The leader can then go out on to the bridge and finish the climb by small ledges on the vertical right wall. Without a threaded rope this finish would be rather risky as the holds are very poor and careful balance is necessary. It is a gully to be recommended for a wet day : while we were in it a storm came on which blotted out first Grasmoor in the distance, and then High Stile close at hand, streaking the combe with sheets of rain, but until we reached the bridge we were kept perfectly dry by the great overhang of the crowning boulder.

The long straight gully near the angle of Eagle Crag—the longest, steepest and most difficult-looking of the climbs on it—was not tried until Whitweek, 1907. I mentioned that on this holiday Botterill bargained for the inclusion of one or two stiff new climbs in our programme, and he did not complain afterwards that we had given him something too easy. He came over from Wastdale to join our party, and we met him on the Scarth Gap track and crossed the shoulder of High Crag into Birkness Combe. At Warn Gill, three days later, the weather was sultry and thundery, but all the early part of the week the hills were white. When we got up to the Combe clouds were gathering round the rocks and soon began to empty themselves upon us. After doing justice to bowls of hot soup and tea prepared by others of the party, Botterill, Dr. Taylor, West and I set off. The lowest part of the climb was up very steep grass, coated with half-melted snow, so that our fingers were fairly numb when we got to the rocks. About 100 feet up we went out on to a ledge on the face, to the left of the chimney, to be able to belay well for a difficult bit of back and foot work above, followed by an awkward corner where the leader needed a shoulder. After five hours of hard work, we were stopped, two-thirds way up, by a 30 ft. cleft with smooth walls and overhanging back. Botterill thought it might be circumvented on the left in better weather, but he tried in vain up the cold, wet rocks, while snow, hail and rain beat down on us in turns. Above the cleft which stopped us there appeared to be another, twice or three times the height and as uncompromising in character. It was not at all easy to retrace our steps, and altogether we were seven hours in the gully.

The two climbs on Eagle Crag, which Sheldon

and I managed to get up, we called Birkness Chimney and Gully, after the hollow which is wrongly marked " Burtness Combe " on the six-inch Ordnance map. Mr. Nelson, of Gatesgarth, told me that Birkness was the proper name, and though the birches on the nab below, which occasioned it, have almost disappeared—like the hazels from Hasness on the opposite side of the Lake—in both places when the upper soil has been removed by a water burst on the hillside, he has found traces of great numbers. Many changes must have taken place here since the names were first bestowed. Scotch firs and larches have replaced the birches and hazels, and are now amongst the finest features of the valley. Eagles of course have long since disappeared from this, as from every other Eagle Crag in Lakeland. Bleaberries and ling would appear to have migrated from the combes on either side of Red Pike, named after them, for they are both more abundant now in Birkness Combe. It is just about 100 years ago that Wordsworth wrote full of distress at the changes which were impending in his beloved Lake country, and denounced, with warmth, the introduction of the larch and to some extent of the Scotch fir, which he thought out of harmony with the spirit of the place; but very few, I think, would now wish them away from Buttermere, where they have grown to be an essential feature. To me the chief changes are in the friends with whom I once climbed on these hills : Craig is far away in South America, Sheldon in India; some have changed or are about to change their state, and might as well be in either of these places now so far as getting a climb with them goes; one of the gentlest and most loveable lies in Loweswater churchyard. But I am wandering from the text. We have now made a complete tour of the valley and have noticed all the more considerable climbs I know of—quite enough, I think, to make good my contention that after Wastdale Head—though no doubt a long way after—Buttermere is one of the best climbing centres in Lakeland.

IN BUTTERMERE PINE WOODS.

VI. SCOUTS AND OUTPOSTS.

THE rougher part of Lakeland has for a long time been a favourite place for the pursuit of a sport known as " man-hunting." Cambridge men principally have been responsible for its introduction and continuance from year to year, but the development of it, in a modified form, under the name of " Scouts and Outposts " is chiefly due to a few members of the Climbers' Club.

The general idea is for a few scouts to attempt to pass through a long line of outposts, details being varied considerably according to the selected goal and number of players. In the game I am about to describe (entirely from my own point of view, as one of the scouts) the goal was the summit of Sca Fell Pike. Five Scouts were to start at 10 a.m., from Wastdale Head, Boot, or Rosthwaite, as each thought best, and, to succeed, they had to reach the goal before 3 p.m. The Captain of the Outposts (25 in number) could post his men as early as he liked, but they had to keep at least three-quarters of a mile from the goal until 2 p.m., except in actual pursuit of a Scout, and every one taking part in the game was supplied with a map showing the position of this three-quarter mile limit. The rules for capture seemed at first sight somewhat arbitrary. A

Scout was to be considered caught if two Outposts, each within 100 yards of him, together called on him to surrender, but to put an Outpost out of action he had to be actually touched by a Scout.

Our plan of operations required considerable discussion. Two of my fellow Scouts were to start from either Boot or Wastdale; the other two were with me at Rosthwaite. Of course very much depended on the weather : if the tops were cloud-covered we had very little doubt of being able to get through almost anywhere, but we had to be prepared for a clear day. Very much also depended on the Outpost Captain's disposition of his men. Would he post them as close as possible to the three-quarter mile limit, or would he send out some of them to watch for us and fall back as we advanced, until they were near enough to their comrades to effect a capture? If the former, he would be able to place his men 170 yards from one another all round the circle, and in that case they could capture us without moving if we tried to pass midway between any two and were seen. But parts of the limiting circle curved across very rocky ground, where we might easily approach unobserved, and either pass between two Outposts unseen or steal on one of them and capture him, in which case, his nearest comrades, being 170 yards away, could give him no assistance and we should have a fair chance of either racing or dodging to the summit. It seemed much more probable, however, that the

WASTDALE

GREAT END FROM GRAINS GILL.

Captain would place his men farther out on points commanding the approaches, with instructions to signal to one another as soon as a Scout had been seen. Now on the side of Sca Fell Pike facing our starting place, the top of Great End forms a perfect post for surveying the approaches. Much the quickest way for us was by the Grains Gill and Esk Hause path, but for several miles this is in full view from Great End. We decided that only one should risk this route. My two Rosthwaite comrades planned a flank movement, going together as quickly as possibly by the Langstrath track to Esk Pike. There they were to separate for crossing the three-quarter mile limit, in the hope that if the line of Outposts were drawn to catch one, the other might get through at the stretch so left undefended. I was to try the Grains Gill route, keeping under cover so far as I could and then round the west shoulder of Great End, crossing the line in the broken ground between the head of Skew Gill and the middle Pike.

For our side the weather turned out as bad as it could be. Looking up the valley we had bright sun in our eyes; looking down, every stone on the hillside miles away seemed to show out sharp and clear. We put on the least conspicuous clothes we could find, but the bright red sash, which we had to wear on one arm as a badge, fairly flamed in the sunshine. It was some consolation that the white sashes of the Outposts would show even more.

The sunshine might be bad for us as Scouts, but in all other respects it was glorious : it flooded with light the fine little stretch of wooded valley between Stonethwaite and Eagle Crag, up which my friends turned to reach Langstrath; it lighted up even the sombre old Seathwaite yews, and made the clear blue pool at Stockley Bridge and all the nameless falls along Grains Gill sparkle with delight as I raced past them. I now began to take cover, trying to keep always out of sight from Great End, but found it no easy matter. Higher, where Grains Gill runs in a ravine, I left the path altogether for the rocky stream-bed, and made but slow progress. At last I reached the corner where the ravine bends sharply to the east, and here I had to leave the Gill to cross the open stretch at the foot of Great End.

This was the critical part of my course. I watched for some time, under cover, for any sign of an Outpost, but could see none. A large party, led by Professor Armstrong, was approaching. I knew that it was making for Cust's Gully, so I waited for some of the men, hoping to escape observation by mixing with them until the foot of their climb was reached. Unluckily for me they elected to have lunch beside a stream, when in the very middle of the open ground, and I had to make a dash for the western shoulder of Great End. I was nearing it when I heard various whistles. I had evidently been seen and probably Outposts were being sent to catch me as I came round the shoulder. I quickly decided that it was no use pushing forwards, and turning, I made straight for the rocks to the left of Cust's Gully. There I could not be seen from either the top of Great End or the sides, where Outposts would probably be placed. I was in full view of anyone near the track between Sprinkling Tarn and Esk Hause, and in crossing a broad patch of snow, which lay all along the foot of the cliff, I could hardly escape detection by any Outpost below, but I felt sure that none was down there and I climbed up the rocks, chuckling at the thought of the men going round the wrong way to meet me. The rocks were easy enough and I was soon two-thirds way up the cliff. Then, to progress, it was necessary to cross a shallow gully. Alas! when I came to try the snow lying in it I found it as hard as ice. At the foot of the cliff it had been soft enough and I had not expected a barrier of this kind. It was impossible to kick steps in it and I had not taken my ice-axe with me. This was very annoying, for it was only about four steps across to rocks which would lead easily to the top, so I tried in a number of places, but it was too much to risk, unroped, and I had to come down about a hundred feet and ascend again closer to the Central Gully. Two or three times I had trouble in circumventing patches of ice, but at last I was just under the top rocks, and peeped stealthily to see if an enemy were in sight. The rounded edge above the cliffs hid the actual summit, but the coast seemed clear, and

I rested under the rock awhile to prepare for a rush across the top of Great End to the three-quarter mile circle, which was now only a quarter of a mile away.

I had not run ten yards up the rounded slope when I came full on an Outpost. The men who had been in touch with him had been sent down to the shoulder to look out for me, so he was helpless to capture me, and he seemed too surprised at my sudden appearance to run away and escape being captured himself. I touched him and called on him to surrender and come with me to the Pike. We proceeded a couple of hundred yards when the Captain of the Outposts appeared trotting towards us and shouted, evidently under the impression that we were two of his men neglecting our duty. I told my prisoner to keep quiet and we went forwards to meet the Captain, but when close to us he recognized his mistake and doubled. I gave chase but soon found that I was no match for him and desisted. The beaten track was quickly reached and the three-quarter mile limit passed. Though I was safe now from meeting any more Outposts the Captain might be able to find another of his men and pursue me, so I pushed on and had the satisfaction of reaching the summit of Sca Fell Pike an hour and a half before the time-limit.

My prisoner proved a most useful acquisition, for his pockets were filled with all kinds of delicacies for lunch while mine were empty. We were able, therefore, to pass the time very agreeably, looking out meanwhile for other Scouts to appear, watching a number of Outposts, who were in sight from the cairn, scouring the country round with their field-glasses, and deriving instruction and amusement from the remarks of numbers of tourists round us. After waiting half an hour two more Scouts advanced together towards us.   They were from Eskdale and had got through the chain near Cam Spout, where they had to grovel along near enough to some Outposts to hear them talk to one another.

Soon the ring of Outposts began to close in, and very curious it looked from the mountain top to see them converging from all directions.   My com-panions from Rosthwaite had not been caught, but their route had been too long and they lost through exceeding the time-limit.   We had won by ten to six—three for each of the three Scouts who had got through and one for the Outpost captured, against three for each of the two Scouts who had failed.

From three to half-past there were between fifty and sixty people on the summit and it was unpleasantly like the top of Snowdon after the arrival of a loaded train.   The impression I brought away was something like this—

" Hel-lo-o ! Come along, it *is* the top this time."

" Eh, but that was warm work; it's a stiff pull up."

" Hel-lo-o-o—o ! ! "

" Well, where's the map ?   Let's see where we

are.   Who are all these fellows with handkerchiefs round their arms? "

" Just a dash of whiskey in it?"   " Careful: don't spill! "

" See, there are some with red ones : whatever have they been doing?"

" Now, that must be the Isle of Man.   Where's the compass? "

" Nay, that's Scotland."

" Have a marmalade—the meat are all finished."

" Now, steady a minute : stand right on the top, and you three make a group in front.   Are you right?   Done."

" Thank goodness that's over.   By Jove, but it's cold; let's get out of the wind."

" Here are some more of them with white hand-kerchiefs."

" Well, how many have got through?   What, three?   Well don't tell me you got through where we were !   And is that one of our men chained up with the rope?   Leave our man alone, will you."

" Nay, never mind the compass, it's not working right.   That's the Isle of Man right enough I tell you.   You say it isn't—well then what is it? "

" Hello, you up here?   how are you?   Scouts and Outposts?   Rather a fool's game, eh? "

" I'd have preferred a climb on a grand day like this, but still it's not bad fun.   What have you been doing? "

" Careful now—there, you've broken it : better try a tin-opener."

" But could you see us when you where crawling past ? "

" Well, that's a relief.   Oh, my poor body and bones.   Isn't there an easier way down ? "

" Here's my mackintosh to sit on, Papa; isn't it grand up here ? "

" Now, keep together, girls, or you'll get lost : come away from that edge !   Oh, it isn't an edge, isn't it ?   Well, come away from it and then you won't fall over."

" Has something glued the bottle fast in that corner ?   Just let it circulate a bit."

" Hcl-lo !   Hell-l-o-o-o—! ! ! . . . . Didn't you hear the echo then ? "

" I can't hear anything with all this rabble round."

" Well, that'll be Helvellyn, with what do they call it—Red Tarn—underneath it."

" That's Windermere man."

" Get along, look at the map : Windermere's not a bit of a thing that shape."

" It is certainly Windermere, with Wansfell above it : I know it very well."

" I told him it were, Mister, but he won't believe nothing from me."

" Never mind Windermere.   What I want to see is the Isle of Man.   When our Bob knows I've been up here the first thing he'll ask is 'Did you see the Isle of Man?' and I don't care whether that's it or the other, but if I've seen the Isle of Man——"

Imagine this sort of thing kept on for nearly an hour, always a dozen people shouting at once, with occasional wild war whoops interspersed, and you may perhaps have some idea of the way we desecrated Sca Fell Pike that afternoon. It was a pleasant contrast (after going down to Wastdale for tea and to meet old friends) to have a quiet walk back to Rosthwaite with the Captain of the Outposts, under the sunset glow on the Napes, and then in the cool stillness of twilight down Borrowdale.

VII. DAYS ON THE PILLAR.

AMONG Lakeland crags the Pillar, though far-famed, can hardly from any standpoint claim supremacy. Doe Crags offer more uniformly difficult climbing; the Napes are incomparably more effective as a distant feature on the mountain side, and none can vie with the cliffs of Sca Fell for grandeur. For me, however, the Pillar holds the first place as the scene of so many happy, although too often unsuccessful struggles. Its grandeur is not of a kind to impress at sight : indeed the first view of it from the Gable top disappointed me. I suppose I must have expected something like the picture of it from Ennerdale Water by J. B. Pyne—a veritable Pillar, separated from the hillside by a vertical notch a thousand feet deep. Vertical it should be, but nearer fifty feet than a thousand on this side, and yet, now, the rock seems grander at every visit, and it is the picture that is disappointing, so little does impressiveness depend on mere height and so much on all that memory adds. That dark line calls up remembrances of all the struggles with its chockstones : that hardly seen ledge brings back visions down great walls of rock and the thrills of excitement that came when it was first traversed, but to many they must be mere streaks of dark or light, " signifying nothing."

I frequently saw the Pillar while rambling over the hills, but never at close quarters until one Easter when I and several other novices had the privilege of accompanying some well-known rock climbers for a first lesson in their sport.

We were to watch them, while they went up the West Way to examine something on the Low Man, after which we were to go round and wait for them at the start of the Easy Way. As we sat lunching at the foot of the unmelted drift which overlay the west scree we wondered how anyone could possibly get up the rock in front of us on this side, The cliff was almost entirely in shadow, showing none of those ledges which appear when the sun slants across it, and looked an almost unbroken vertical wall. Its outline is most imposing on this side; the rock rises proudly for the first 400 feet; then the line is interrupted by the Low Man platform, from which the High Man springs up again in a fine parabolic sweep, suddenly terminated on the south west by a vertical drop of 200 feet. The upper quarter of this drop is one side of the notch which isolates the rock while the lower 150 feet forms a wall of the blackest and in some ways the most imposing gully on the Pillar—at that time unclimbed and thought unclimbable.

We watched our elders rope and start and were surprised at the rapidity with which they went along and up places which looked appallingly perilous and steep. I was still more surprised a year or two

THE PILLAR, LOW MAN.

CLOUD WREATHS ON THE PILLAR

later, when I went over the climb myself, to find what a fraud it was—ledges in abundance and hardly a place where the hands are needed. The rock faces to right and left of it, however, are the finest on the Pillar.

When our companions turned the corner of the High Man we retraced our steps and waited on the east side. How great, looming through the mists of ignorance, does many an insignificant climb appear. Here we were at last about to start on a task which had baffled even a President of the Alpine Club. Only a few yards from where we stood a man had once slipped and was dashed to pieces, &c., &c. Such was the melodramatic, popular magazine and half-penny paper way of viewing the world which, I think, predominated while we were waiting, all nervously excited, until our friends appeared, rounding the ledge, and Mr. Fowler changed ropes and started up again with us. Another party was coming down by the " ledge " route, so our leader took us straight up the " curtain." The first surprise, on reaching it, was to see, on the other side, a well-known venerable-looking Professor running about over these danger-ous rocks unroped, and the second was to find even the steepest places perfectly easy, in spite of a sharp little snowstorm which enlivened the ascent. In-deed, our only difficulty was in suppressing one of our number, who would persist in offering advice to an experienced leader of another party. Except when the rocks are badly coated with snow and ice, the ascent by any of the variations of the " Easy Way " is very simple—so easy in fact that my youngster led up when ten years old without any help beyond an indication of the route—an important reservation, some of the early Pillarites might suggest.

Next to the climb itself the most interesting event of the day was an examination of the double tin box on the top, when we added our cards to the pile according to custom.   They have all gone now, the noted names along with the unknown.   A year or two ago one of my friends found half of the inner box down in the West Jordan Gully, blown over in some storm apparently, and remains of some cards were picked up on the Fells.   Luckily the piece of slate is still preserved on which climbers scratched their names in the early days, before the advent of the tin box : it ought surely to be in the possession of the Alpine or Climbers' Club.

A couple of years elapsed after this first visit before I saw the Pillar again.   In the meantime I had been busy, as opportunity offered, on the Gable and Sca Fell, and now I thought of trying the north face.   It is done so frequently to-day, and the way is so unmistakably marked, that much of its repute has gone, but in those days it was thought one of the most difficult things on the Pillar.   My brother and I were setting out for it from the Inn when George Abraham told us that two parties were already bound for the same climb, and suggested that we might all go together. The result was that we took part in a long and heterogenous procession up Mosedale. We had representatives of experience in Eckenstein and George Abraham—the one of mountaineering generally, the other of the rock and district; at the other end of the scale came my brother and I; the genial librarian of the Climbers' Club brought with him his wife and a friend, and our cavalcade included also the venturesome Puttrell and W. R. Reade who had just made a name for himself by the first ascents of Twll Du and the West Jordan Gully. It was as well that we had with us some who knew the lie of the land, for after crossing Lookingstead into Ennerdale we got into cloud and saw little more for the rest of the day. The high level track was not well defined then, and I have known people who have been unable to find the Pillar without going first to the top of the Fell. In thick mist I have even walked right past the foot of the rock without knowing it, until brought up by the waterfall on the west side.

We roped in two parties: George Abraham led one by what is known as the "stomach traverse" route; the other, which I joined, was led by Reade, who took the westerly variation. We never saw more than a few feet of the rock at once, and the only idea I got of the grandeur of the climb was given by the general angle at which we ascended. Though steep, however, the rocks are well broken up, and there is no really awkward problem until a ledge 300 feet up is reached. Here the two routes meet and we found the other party waiting for us, to rearrange the forces. The two leaders joined and descended into Savage Gully—" stooping to conquer," as Mr. Haskett-Smith, the inventor of the route aptly describes the manœuvre. They then unroped from us and made a long détour, whilst we, seated together on a good platform, followed the advice " Make use of time; let no advantage slip." Our lunch was finished before we heard above us the voices of our leaders who threw down a rope to which we tied, and continued the ascent in one long string. The first move we had to make was certainly the most sensational piece of rock climbing I had seen up to that time. It was round and up the " Nose," a fairly smooth lump of rock about 10 feet high, which bellied out, overhanging a gully whose floor descended steeply into the mist. It looked very alarming, even with the rope held by two good men above, to see one after another stand balancing on a mere spike of rock near the verge of our platform, with no apparent handhold, while the left knee was raised cautiously on to a ledge, invisible to us, round the projecting mass. However, looks are often very deceptive : there is a most thrilling looking photograph of some climbers traversing the " Ledge," one of the easiest bits on the " Easy Way " up the Pillar, and the present problem, though awkward enough, proved not so bad as it looked. In the many discussions there have been as to the best number on one rope I have never seen nine suggested as an ideal. I have heard of a party of 13 going up Kern Knotts Chimney. The first few men were able to unrope at the top and come down to offer advice to those of their comrades who were impatiently waiting to start, but apart from special advantages of this kind, which may not appeal to every one, the frequent opportunities for admiring the scenery on good days or for raillery and anecdote on bad ones, are the only recommendations I can think of. The number did not come amiss that day at least: Eckenstein was next to me on the rope and enlivened the waits with the raciest of stories about his many friends and enemies amongst men and mountains, and the four or five hours which we must have taken over the ascent, passed rapidly enough. It was a good climb— interesting and long, without too much exertion— and I looked forward to the next visit to Lakeland, for an opportunity to repeat it in clear weather, and compare the reality with what the imagination had built up from the bits into a glorious whole.

I set out for it next on a lovely June morning, this time from Keswick, with Craig. Blue shadows lay softly amongst the hills and there were many temptations to lie down—under the fresh green foliage amongst the uncurling croziers of bracken in Newlands, by the pine woods along Buttermere, and again beside the river in Ennerdale, so that it was

two o'clock before we reached the Pillar foot. I
thought it would be interesting to take the Stomach
Traverse route this time, and we quickly climbed the
lower indefinite portion of Savage Gully to where
the route strikes away from it to the right. Then a
wild idea came into my head. Above us was the
part of Savage Gully which had never been climbed
—about which I had heard so much discussion at
Wastdale Head—which led straight to the top of
the Low Man without any zigzaging or descending
manœuvres. Why should we not try it? It was
rather mad for us, with our small experience, to
attempt what many well-known men had tried and
pronounced impossible, but we stuck at it for a long
time and alternately gave one another some alarming
views of nailed boot soles high and almost vertically
above. We managed 40 or 45 feet of the unclimbed
gully, but could do no more, and we turned back to
content ourselves with the accustomed route. We
reached the Nose without difficulty, and I descended
the Savage Gully crack. Then I began to wonder
which way to go. On the previous occasion I was
not near enough to the edge to watch the leaders'
tactics. There was a perfectly easy traverse to the
east, but I soon ran out the length of the rope on it.
Craig could not follow me, the descent into Savage
Gully being too risky without a rope above, so I
tried to climb straight up the Gully on to the " Nose "
—I knew it was not the usual way, but it had been
done several times before. Just as I was pulling

NORTH FACE OF THE PILLAR

WEST FACE OF THE PILLAR, HIGH MAN

over the top jammed stone my hands slipped on
some greasy rock and down I went. Craig had firm
hold of the rope, but he was some thirty feet away,
round the " Nose," and after a rapid and exhilarating
descent I swung down the gully like a pendulum and
came back against the rock with a bang. It was one
of those incidents which strengthen friendships, but
which nevertheless I am not anxious to repeat. My
cap came off in the fall, and we found it later in the
day, 300 feet below, at the base of the rock. Craig
escaped with a finger scraped by the rope; I suffered
even less, and was ready for another try in a few
minutes. This time I tried a little to the left of the
gully, but without success, and I climbed back to
Craig up the crack. He repeated my tactics
(omitting the aërial flight), and ended by returning
to the ledge beside me. We looked at one another
and laughed. It was decidedly ignominious to be
beaten by the North Climb after daring to imagine
that we might conquer Savage Gully, but the fact
was plain enough, and we had to make up our minds
to descend as we had come up. I don't know
whether we were more consoled or maddened at
finding out, not so long after, that we had really got
over all the difficulties, and that either of us might
have unroped, walked round by the traverse we had
seen, helped the other over the " Nose," and to the
Pillar top without any trouble. Well, I at least had
gone largely for a good view of the rock's north face,
and we had got that without a doubt. For five or

six hours we had been overshadowed by the walls of Savage Gully or the cliffs above the Strid, and it gave us both such a delight in the climb that we have repeated it oftener than any other. We had been reckless of the time and darkness overtook us before we reached Scarth Gap, but we were in no hurry to tear ourselves away from the fleshpots of Buttermere, so delicious was everything after our long day; and we reached Keswick well after midnight. "What miserable 'valley-pounding,'" do I hear some climbers say? Well, I admit that Keswick is not a good base from which to attack the Pillar. At the same time, I have no sympathy with the ever-increasing number who look on the tramp to the foot of the crags as "a beastly grind." It will be disastrous to the sport of climbing if its devotees cease to love the mountains as a whole, as the older men did, and wish only for the crags.

Happily the finest Lakeland climbs are all out of the way on the hill-tops, and the tramps to them are delightful preludes, amongst which none are finer or more varied than that from Buttermere to the Pillar. The first stretch, although along the high road, is through a world of romance where (except at the mid-day hour when coaches hurry past) elfin music seems ever to dwell. Bits of rugged mountain side come and go between the tall fir tops; a squirrel peeps and twinkles off behind an ivy-strangled mast which raises its thin tassels high into the golden sunshine overhead. Beneath, amongst mossy stones, a stream tosses down in the half-luminous green gloom towards the lake, and ahead is always the grand hollow of Warnscale. Then, after the Gatesgarth meadows, and a little exercise of muscles up to Scarth Gap, comes the sudden view of the Gable cliffs, and soon after, round the edge of the near crag on the right, the Pillar itself appears with Pillar Fell like the crest of a breaking wave above it. A wild run down the grassy slope; a steady pull up the opposite side; the last of the many rocky humps is rounded, and the north face of the Pillar fronts us, ready for battle.

Off goes Craig's cap, with a hearty hail of " How do, old Pillar."

Irreverent? Rather the familiarity of affection for the rock which has defeated us, how often? Ever a delight to re-visit, but all the more enjoyed for the expectance and the spin of the blood evoked by the healthy tramp.

Then on the way back we can take the bridle path through the pine woods on the opposite side of Buttermere and tramp noiselessly in the twilight on the cushioned pine needles, with glimpses of the Lake gleaming between gaunt stems : or if Wastdale is our destination there is always the chance that we may see a flood of light striking over Mosedale until it fires Sca Fell cliffs with a ruddy glow, as we descend in the shadow. But even apart from sights we would miss something good if we had not the preliminary stretching of the legs and the final helter-skelter down the rough hill-side.

The next time that Craig and I attacked the Pillar we took everything quietly : sauntered lazily upwards from Wastdale to the drowsy noise of grasshoppers on the hot turf; climbed the Central and West Jordan Chimneys, Pendlebury Traverse, and variations of the Easy Way; went down the North Climb to the place which we reached the time before, and saw what we ought to have done; basked for an hour on the Low Man, reducing the plentiful crop of bilberries, and strolled back to meet our friend Tom Shaw, who was to join us in a second attack on Savage Gully the next day.

The Wastdale dinner failed to exert the same magnetic influence on him that it had on us. He arrived a day late, having missed his train connection, lost his luggage, broken his bicycle on an atrocious road, had various other delays and mishaps, and, to crown all, he brought the pleasing intelligence that he would have to be back at Wastdale the next day in time to drive down, pick up his damaged bicycle from some lonely farmhouse, and catch the evening train at Seascale. There was little chance of giving proper attention to Savage Gully that day, but we had good sport out of a repetition of the North Climb, and got Shaw down in time to keep his appointment.

A year elapsed before we made another attempt. Our party was the same with the addition of a friend from the south, Gerald West. This time we had everything in our favour—a calm day, dry rocks, and warm sunshine—and our hopes were great. West had never climbed before in England, and he thought we were making game of him when we got opposite the rock and pointed the way up, but difficulties usually dwindle when they are attacked. The tops of the organ pipes, of which the north face appears in certain lights to be composed, make splendid platforms, and it is generally easy to pass from one of these to another slightly higher at the angle between two pipes. Savage Gully is almost lost amongst all these vertical lines of rock : instead of the typical Cumberland gully, like Walker's close by, with chock-stones prominent against its black recesses, we have a shallow channel, rising up 120 feet from where the North Climb leaves it, without a ledge which will accommodate more than the toes; without any opposing walls to back up against; without any jammed stones to break up the ascent. At the top of this 120 feet there is a moderately good resting-place, and above that, steep water-rounded slabs up to the crack where the North Climbs joins it once more. Shaw and West climbed to the top of one of the organ pipes overlooking the gully, and held the rope from there while Craig and I made the attempt. We tried hard, and reached a point 10 feet higher than before, but beyond this we could see no way, and acknowledged ourselves beaten, with everything in our favour. Looking back now, the one thing we regret is that Shaw did not match himself against the gully. He had hardly shewn what he could do then : judging by his deeds since, I believe he would have climbed it that day.

Having failed in our attempt, we turned towards the North Climb, which we were beginning to hail as an old friend. To West it was something new and undreamed of. His appreciation was unbounded, though mixed with apprehension at times when we disappeared round the famous Stomach Traverse, or invited him to join us above the Nose, or lead the way down the Central Jordan chimney. Very few people like the look of the descent by this route the first time they see it : after they have been up and down once or twice they begin to find it the quickest way to or from the Pillar and one of the neatest little climbs on the rock. I can still see West disappearing over the edge, his face turned up in an agonized way.

" Have you got me ? I feel in a most precarious position."

"We could hold tons from here : just 'clasp that crag with crooked hands,' as you've been spouting all day, and let yourself gently down."

Then a deep voice answers, "'And like a thunderbolt he falls,'" and a minute later his face is looking up from the base of the rock, beaming with pleasure at having accomplished so easily what looked so impossible. He strolled off at his ease towards Wastdale while we turned back for some more scrambling. As we left the Pillar that evening it and the Shamrock towering up together against the descending pomp of light seemed to shout defiance at us. We stood long, fascinated by the rock, which grew darker and more inaccessible-looking every minute. At last a raven floated off from the top and circled round with a hoarse mock of a cry. It sounded like a jeer at our defeat, and we laughed and retreated homewards thinking of the luxuries West had promised himself and would be then enjoying—tea with a thin slice of lemon floating over it, to be sipped while half-dozing in a hot bath. Climbers are a queer mixture of extremes : though they do get through the day on a meagre fare of jam sandwiches and raisins, they are veritable sybarites after the hard work is over.

While we had been trying in vain to overcome Savage Gully, other parties had been more successful in the exploration of the Pillar. Since my first climb on the rock Reade and McCulloch had found a way up the West Jordan Gully; Walker's Gully had, after many attempts, been conquered by a strong trio led by O. G. Jones; and an intricate way had been worked out by the Abraham brothers up some of the finest rocks on the west side of the High Man.

A day or two after the last climb had been accomplished Craig and I were at Wastdale, and the Thompsons of Cardiff, who had been doing great things there, suggested that we should try a second ascent together. Craig unluckily felt unfit in the morning and decided on an off-day. The rest of us set out, armed with a full description and sketch of the climb, copied out of the Wastdale book. These we studied carefully whilst we had lunch, with the rock in front of us to refer to. The diagram was clear enough, though, as we identified the route on the Pillar itself many details could not be made to agree with the description. We understood that the climb was sensational, but the one shewn on the sketch was clearly impossible, and we decided to rely on the notes alone. The start was soon found, and Philip Thompson led up rapidly. It was not long before we seemed to be half-way to the top, but difficulties had begun: we could go no further directly upwards, and a traverse was not feasible. We had evidently missed the first traverse, and descended some distance to find it. Once found we climbed without much difficulty to the second traverse about which there could be no mistake. The situation here is magnificent: a steep rib has been followed until it ends against a vertical wall. Ten feet away horizontally there is a small grassy patch at the foot of a chimney by which the ascent must be continued. Ten feet seems little enough to traverse, but the chasm which must be crossed gives a glimpse downwards which makes the climber thank the designer of the Pillar fervently for a belaying pin which offers itself just where it is most needed. The rock above the ledges on which the traverse must be made projects in such a way as to make standing upright impossible. The first party crawled, but we noticed a chain of capital holds along the ledge, and made the passage by a hand traverse, the body swinging free. The chimney, which starts from the grass patch to which we crossed, ends above in a cave overhung by large blocks. We all gathered here and prospected for the third traverse, which took some finding, for the rocks were very slightly scratched then. The situation of the leader as he stepped round the corner was quite sensational, but when our turn came it was found to be not so bad. After this an easy scramble led us to the top of what is, in my opinion, the most interesting and enjoyable climb, for its height (only about 250 feet) in Lakeland. The discoverers deserve great credit for having worked out such an intricate way up one of the most unpromising-looking rock faces on the Pillar, and one which, although full of sensational situations, is nevertheless, if the rope is properly managed, perfectly safe.

Craig had recovered his wonted vigour and spirits when we returned, and I had a few days' most enjoyable climbing with him, after which I was left alone at Wastdale with Peter Thompson. He had heard of all our attempts on Savage Gully, and, as he was feeling very fit, proposed that we should try it as a good finish to the holiday. I joyfully acquiesced, and we decided this time to explore it first from above. We set out with a large quantity of rope, and were soon at the " Nose " ready to start operations. Thompson put on scarpetti and

began the descent.   The first part was well known
and went quickly : then came the water-rounded
slabs, from which, steadied by the rope above, he
removed earth or grass wherever these had lodged
in any crack that might be of use.   Lower down
were the chief difficulties, and for a long time signals
to pull in or let out the rope alternated, while every
now and then a quantity of loose stuff would be seen
careering down the steep ground below the foot of
the Pillar.   At length the signals for letting out
more rope ceased, and I took it in slowly but steadily
until Thompson was once more beside me.

"It will go," he said, "but—" and the ellipsis was
more eloquent than words.

We went down the West Way, crossed the waterfall
and started at the foot of Savage Gully.   I was
interested to see how Thompson would proceed when
he reached the highest point I had climbed to.   He
also could get no further straight ahead, but he
managed to make a most daring traverse across a
rib which divides the shallow back of the gully, after
which he was able to continue the ascent.   He was
getting so high above me that the rope was rapidly
becoming more of a dangerous impediment than a
safeguard, but no resting-place revealed itself until
110 feet of rope were out.   I then attempted to
follow, but the traverse about 60 feet up was too
difficult for me, and I slipped off.   Before trying
again, I enquired about the difficulties higher up.
Thompson had climbed the lower portion rather

differently, crossing the rib two or three times, and when I shouted that I had come off on the first traverse he replied that another higher up was very much worse. I found out afterwards that I had been at the severest piece of the climb, but at the time, thinking there was worse to follow, I foolishly decided not to try again. Then followed a council of war. The upper part, though not so difficult, was dangerous, and I offered to go up the North Climb to the Nose and drop a rope to Thompson for safety. The soles of his scarpetti had been so filled up with earth during the preliminary explorations that he had discarded them, and put on his boots, but he thought the upper slabs would be safer in stockings, and sent his boots down to me on the rope. I got up to the Nose as rapidly as I could with the encumbrance of 200 feet of rope round my shoulders and a pair of climbing boots dangling from the end of it. Now and then I had qualms of conscience, for a knew I was not following the recognized rules of the sport : several times before I had done similar climbs alone, and after each time had said " never again." However, I knew the North Climb well, and had little fear of any mishap on it. Arrived at the Nose, I let down the rope for Thompson, who also had taken risks and climbed considerably higher. To disarm cavillers the rope was not taken in as he climbed up until he reached me, when we hurried on to the summit of the rock and I con-gratulated him on having accomplished the first ascent of the most difficult climb on the Pillar, which had attracted the attention of many of the best mountaineers for the previous 10 or 15 years. Thompson confessed that he wouldn't care to repeat it, and that he had found it worse than either the Eagle's Nest Arête or Slanting Gully, but it had been done at last. Of course I was very disappointed at my own failure, but it was some consolation to have helped at the conquest, and we had a merry evening, after a day of "aching joys and dizzy raptures" long to be remembered.

It must be admitted that Savage Gully is hardly a legitimate climb : a slip on the part of the leader at the most difficult place would probably prove fatal, and none of my friends were very anxious to try it when we next visited the Pillar. On the other hand, all wanted to have a look at the new West Wall climb. It was a day such as does not come more than once in a twelvemonth, the day on which Edward VII. was to have been crowned, and a truly fitting Coronation Day it would have been. The whole district was revelling in sunshine, laughing with the delight of life and freshness. We drank the King's health beside the west waterfall, and then roped up in two parties of three. I was appointed to lead, and could hardly believe that it was the same climb, so much easier was everything, with dry warm rocks. There was no doubt about the route this time, and in an hour and a half after the start we were at the top of the climb, which all pronounced one of the most enjoyable in Lakeland.

My wife was waiting for us on the fell, and I descended, to take her up the Pillar for the first time by the Easy Way. When we reached the top we found the others doing a risky-looking little climb to the east of the Jordan Gap. It turned out that a gentleman had walked over to the foot of the Pillar and shouted up to them asking which way they had come up. They, thinking he had asked the way up, had shewn him the Easy Way. Their confusion later may be imagined, when they found the supposed novice knew more about the Pillar than any of us! He was Mr. Geoffrey Hastings, and in return for their information he showed them Haskett-Smith's Extreme-East Jordan route, which they were finishing when my wife and I reached them. All the little climbs followed : the many variations of the Easy way, Pendlebury's traverse, the Pendlebury corner, the West and Central Jordan chimneys and so on, all taken quietly and varied by lying drowsily on the Pillar top, heedless of the fact that dinner at Wastdale was commencing. What did dinner matter in such weather; we had it at nine the night before—this evening it would be at ten. We continued in the same happy heedlessness of time after dinner was over and sat outside, listening to Mr. Robinson's stories of the conquests ten year's earlier, while the twilight circled round from Red Pike and the Steeple towards Black Sail, until dawn began to make the stars look wan.

" Rest after toyle, port after stormy seas, ease

after war, death after life doth greatly please " and there is something to be said also in favour of the pleasures of hardship and a strenuous life after being sated with ease. We had opportunity to properly appreciate these on our next visit to the Pillar under cold January skies, the rocks sheeted over with ice, and the fell-tops just frosted to a steely grey. As we came along the high level, Shamrock Gully straight in front attracted us. There is no real climbing in the lower part, but some care had to be taken under the wintry conditions, and our hands were fairly numbed by the ice, which was in that unpleasant, rounded, slightly melting state which seems to chill more than hard frost. As there is only one proper pitch we chose the more difficult of the two ways up it, and very difficult we found it. We rubbed our hands well with snow to restore the circulation before starting, but all feeling had gone long before we reached the top slab which we found covered with a smooth sheet of ice and requiring the greatest care. There was no dawdling about on the Pillar top this time when we had finished : a hasty bite, and then off at a trot to reach Looking Stead before dark, for a late start from Wastdale had played havoc with the short winter day.

Three months later we paid the Pillar another visit from Buttermere, and found it still looking wintry, though the frost was giving way quickly and as we plodded slowly up we saw several falls of hanging ice curtains. Dr. Sheldon, Craig, and I thought of attacking Walker's Gully, while the other three in our party went to the West Jordan Gully. We washed down our lunch with icy cold water coming down the gully, which gave a premonition of what we should have to encounter. We took some time considering the best way to attack the first pitch. Three routes seemed possible. One was that adopted by Jones who made the first ascent and lay to the left of the gully : another was up the right wall inside the gully; the third by the chimney at the very back of the cleft. The third way seemed the most honourable, but, that day at least, the water streaming over half-melted ice on the smooth walls made it quite impracticable. We decided on the second course and Sheldon led us up what proved the most dangerous part of the climb. The top of the pitch was one of those deceptive places which look so easy to those below that they can't make out why the leader doesn't go on until they get spread out in the same position themselves and find they need an extra arm or leg. Above this first big pitch the chockstones are numerous and close together. A green one, half way up, very noticeable from below, gave us some trouble, and higher still there was an awkward hole to wriggle through, but all difficulties lower down seemed as nothing to what confronted us when we reached the final pitch. The type is not at all an uncommon one in Cumberland : for standing place a ledge close to the top of a nearly vertical cleft, under a roof formed by large jammed boulders. As a rule such obstacles can be passed by backing up, or scrambling on the side walls, or squeezing through a hole behind the boulder. Here there is no escape at the back, and the gully is too wide for backing up until near the top. The only possible way is up one of the side walls, and both these overhang. Our prospects of success were small, but the climb had been done three times before and Sheldon was determined that it should be done again. In order to pass out from under the roof it was necessary to traverse some distance—further on the right wall than on the left, but Sheldon chose the former for the attempt because the holds, bad as they were, seemed slightly the better. The rope was threaded behind a boulder above and then Sheldon started. He got out of the shadow of the roof and a little way up. Then he stuck for some time, holding on to a slight knob with one hand, unable to move on or back. It seemed a great exertion for him merely to stay where he was and at last his foot slipped off its tiny sloping ledge and down he came, hanging like a spider from the roof. I held the rope tight while Craig pulled him back into the cave, and then he lit his pipe and considered the problem once more. Twice again he tried and swung off, dangling in mid-air; then he declared himself too exhausted to try again. Neither Craig nor I offered to lead, knowing too well that where Sheldon failed we should have no chance. Just then one of our party appeared at the bottom of the gully, shouldering the rücksack, which he was about to take round to the others on the Pillar top, and we asked if they would help us out with a rope from above before they left.

We settled ourselves for a half-hour's rest and began to take stock of the rather limited view. Directly beneath us was a drop of 100 feet; then over a jammed stone there was the scree at the gully foot, looking about half-way down to the river, although in reality only about 200 feet out of 2,000. On the other side of the river our attention was attracted by an unwonted sight—a cart—for there was no road, only a rough footpath up the valley. Two men were throwing something out of it,— planks apparently from the noise they made as they fell on one another, for although we heard nothing of the doings of our friends on the Pillar close above us, we could distinctly hear all manner of little sounds in the valley below, a mile away—even the murmur of the river at times.

At length the cart was emptied and rumbled downwards out of our field of view, leaving us to speculate on the meaning of the intrusion. (A few months later we found the planks clamped together and thrown across a tiny rill to form a bridge; the old track being transformed into a miry road up to some sheepfolds at the head of Ennerdale.) The shoulder between High Stile and High Crag curling round to the summit of the former, and revealing as

it curled upwards just an indication of the rocky
hollow it concealed, began to look tiresomely
familiar, and it was in some ways a welcome change
to see a cloud pass over and leave the top white.
Soon filmy white curtains appeared between us and
the opposite fell side, falling slowly and drifting up
the valley, and in a few more minutes we were in the
middle of a snowstorm. We were too well sheltered
by our boulder roof to be much inconvenienced,
except by the cold, and enjoyed watching the
curious behaviour of the nearer flakes which were
blown vertically upwards past us by a constant eddy
of wind in the gully. Craig merrily sang over again
the songs of the previous evening, of which a verse
from the " Tarpaulin Jacket " struck us as the most
appropriate—

> " Oh had I the wings of a little dove—little dove,
>   Far, far away would I fly—I fly, &c."

Sheldon meanwhile was busy perfecting an appli-
ance for attaching to the rope between each pair of
climbers—a sort of self-registering pressure-guage
which would ring once for " moral support," twice
for pulling up by main force, three times for sudden
and unexpected descents, &c. He might have
retaliated when we wanted to know how many rings
would stand to his account that day, but he forbore.

At last, long after the half-hour we had reckoned
on had passed, we heard footsteps on the scree just
above us and a friendly rope was let down. Our

comrades had hard work to get us out. We climbed as far as we could : then we would shout that the rope might be used at any moment : it would be pulled tight and would drag us off our little holds at once. Next would come a swing out into space, with perhaps a spin round in the air, and those above would have to pull hard until we could clutch at something to help ourselves with.

When we got out the snow had stopped falling. Very little daylight was left and we had to make the best use of it to get down and across the river. It was a mad helter-skelter down over boulders and holes hidden by the fresh soft snow, which however gave us some light, for on reaching the lower slopes, where it had melted, we seemed suddenly to plunge into the dark. The river was crossed, and then we threw ourselves down on the grass and prepared for a good meal.

That hour beside the stream lingers in my memory : we were ravenously hungry and by good chance the rücksack had been filled by a pair of epicures. The people at Buttermere knew enough by experience of our unpunctual habits to have no anxiety at our absence from the dinner table, so we lay at our ease. The rücksack was emptied at last, but still we lay stretched out on the cold hillside listening to the river beside us. Nothing was to be seen now but the friendly glow of pipe and cigarette, and the mountain wall rimming us round, darker than the dark sky, until a fairy glimmer crept

upwards behind Great Gable. In half an hour more
the full moon was flooding Ennerdale with light
and helping us over pitfalls and stumbling blocks
on our homeward tramp.

Craig and I were glad at heart : we had climbed
as much of Walker's Gully as we were ever likely
to be able to do, had a glorious day, and were
content; not so Sheldon. He worried all the next
day, which we devoted to a hill ramble, and we
returned to Walker's Gully the day after. We had
found that one man was quite sufficient to look after
the rope and Craig generously offered to stand out
and join the other party on the Pillar. This time
Sheldon chose the left hand route up the first pitch
and we found it much easier : the remainder was all
familiar and we were soon up to the great pitch.
Here Sheldon took off his coat and boots and tried
his stockings on the iced ledges. They gripped
well and after a rest and a pipe he set off in light
attire. In what seemed less than a minute he was
up at the top, shouting triumphantly. His boots
and coat followed on the rope and I later on in the
same manner.

It is a grand climb, and to be recommended to
any strong and experienced climber—difficult all
the way and at the top extremely difficult, and yet,
if properly tackled, safe throughout.

A very good foretaste of it can be got by doing
the West Jordan Gully. It is only half the height
but the traverse out from the great cave at the top

is quite difficult and exposed enough to make the climb an exciting one. The left wall, on which the traverse has to be made, though not overhanging as in Walker's Gully, is quite vertical, but the holds are just as small, the traverse out longer, and after getting clear of the cave roof, there is still a chimney to climb to get above it. It is strange that so few people go there, for it it is a remarkably fine gully either to look at or out from. Another difficult climb, hereabouts, which is very rarely done, is the Shamrock Chimney. An unkind suggestion has been made that this is due to its omission from the classified list in Mr. Jones's book, so that climbers cannot have the pleasure of ticking it off. Still another not very popular route is that by the Great Chimney, which can be combined very well with the North Climb by leaving Savage Gully above the Nose, where the interest of the climb is over, and scrambling over easy ground to the foot of the curtain.

After speaking of ascents by routes as difficult as those of the West Jordan Gully and Shamrock Chimney, it seems disgraceful to have to record a failure to get up the Pillar by one of the very easiest ways—the West Route, by which it was first climbed in 1826. When we set out from Buttermere on All Fools day, 1904, we had something much bigger than that in our minds—the exploration of a new climb. We had noticed a slight sprinkling of snow on the crest of the High Stile range, but it wasn't

until we were at the top of Scarth Gap that we saw
what the higher mountains were like. On the Pillar
the snow was piled up thickly wherever it could lie,
and the steep parts stood out dark against a white
upper world which faded into green just below the
base of the rock.

Though exploration was out of the question, it
was just the right time for tracing out the best
ledges, by the snow lying on them, and we studied
the rock well from the North, after which we thought
we might as well go up it by the West and down one
of the South ways. We had only one ice-axe
amongst three, and soon found in crossing the rough
slopes before we reached the rock, that we were
going to have trouble. The snow was melting
quickly, and very uneven in thickness, having
drifted into all the hollows, so that at one step we
would sink deeply in, and, at the next, slip off some
sloping iced rock close to the surface. I had very
often before been up and down by the West way and
thought I knew every step of it, but the thickness of
the covering was most misleading and its treacherous-
ness necessitated great caution. When we got half
way from the Low Man to the top of the Pillar we
began to realise that the sun had set. We had
started late, wasted time in examining the rock, and
taken something like three hours over a scramble
which in summer needs only occupy a few minutes.
We turned back and had to flounder most of the way
home in the dark, and I lost the tips of three fingers
from frostbite as a result of that day's adventure.

The new climb which we intended to explore on this last occasion was one which had attracted my attention a good deal the previous summer, when I stayed at Gatesgarth and paid different visits to the Pillar with my wife or boy. We took everything very easily and had plenty of long rests facing the North and West fronts of the rock. Careful scrutiny during these halts gave some promise of the existence of a North-West passage between these two faces, and Sheldon, when he joined us soon after, needed very little persuasion to induce him to spend a day or two in exploration.

We had often enough looked up at the North-West angle admiringly as an unassailable corner of the grand rock; but, until the Abrahams made their West Wall climb, we had looked in just the same way at that part, and although the height of the cliff there is only 250 feet it has always appeared to me more threatening than the much higher North-West corner of the Low Man. The latter varies greatly in its appearance of inaccesibility. Most climbs look worst when seen *en face*—the North Climb, for instance, viewed in this way, appears to run up the sides of vertical columns or across from one which looks bad to another which seems no better; but in profile these columns are seen to have been pushed back every here and there so that the face is dotted all about with fair sized level platforms. The North-West angle is very different from this. The top of a buttress, which stands out here and rises to a third of the way up the Low Man, looks attainable from most points of view and had in fact been reached 13 or 14 years before by Mr. Haskett-Smith. The 300 feet above this, from below shows numerous rather rounded ledges, but when seen in profile from either East or West they seem to have disappeared and various little overhangs not noticed from below show up on the sky line instead.

We made out two different routes where we thought there might be a chance. Both of them looked worst not far below where the cliff joins the broken ground which occupies the upper 60 or 70 feet of the Low Man, and we thought it would be best to look at these places first from the top. We started rather to the West side of the angle and got down to about 130 feet from the Low Man top. Below this the crag looked impossible and we made our way back to try the other route. We found what we thought to be the top of this and got down to a place where further descent seemed equally hopeless, after which we went over the top of the Pillar by the Great Chimney. On our way back, however, we had another good scrutiny, and found that we had made the second attempt at the wrong place—too far to the East.

The next day we found the right place and saw that there was a choice of two chimneys by which one of the steepest parts could be descended; but the weather was too boisterous to try. Poor Sheldon was very disappointed; it was his last chance before leaving for India, but he consoled himself with the West Jordan Gully, the most difficult and exciting of the short climbs on the Pillar, and hoped that the North-West corner would still be unconquered when he returned.

A year later I was again in the district with Messrs. Fox and Spencer, but we had again bad weather. Spencer and I descended the chimney nearest the angle, and traversing to the East to the foot of the other chimney I thought I could make out a route for some distance further, after which we decided to try and reach the place from below as soon as a good opportunity occurred.

However, the next time I went to Wastdale I found that the climb had nearly been accomplished by Messrs. F. Botterill and W. Palmer who, more sportsman-like than myself, had started from the bottom without any prospecting and had got 300 feet up. When they described to me that evening the place they had reached I felt sure that the route had been discovered. They had climbed the buttress without difficulty, and then, working first slightly to the left in ascending and then slightly back again to the right they had got up to within a very few feet of the place we had reached from above. In spite of so nearly accomplishing the climb, however, they could see no way out, and had to descend,—to my mind the most difficult thing done in working out the the climb. I persuaded them to have another try, and two days later they set out again, this time accompanied by Dr. J. H. Taylor, while several of my friends came with me to the Low Man, and secured me while I waited at the top of the chimney furthest of the two from the North-West angle, a good place from which either to see the climb below or to lower a rope if needed. The general angle below may be judged from the fact that in getting the rope ready I accidentally dislodged a stone, which fell within a foot or two of Dr. Taylor who was on the top of the buttress. Unluckily rain came on and made the rocks in bad condition and when the party got up to 130 feet from me (80 feet from the place I had reached before) they decided to ask for our rope. On the previous occasion Botterill and Palmer had got higher than they were now, but had struck off to the right. They now tried to come straight up to the platform at the foot of the chimney below me. For 35 or 40 feet they managed well; then they got into difficulties on some overhanging rocks just below the platform and had to make use of our rope. Dr. Taylor then tried by working more to the left at the start and succeeded in reaching the platform without using the rope. And so the way throughout was discovered and all that remained was to do the climb properly.

The weather was bad the next day: the day following was the end of the holidays, and it was a year later before the climb was again attempted.

On June 8th, 1906, Mr. Fred Botterill, his brother Arthur, Dr. J. H. Taylor, and I had the good luck to make the first successful ascent. We were extremely sorry that Palmer was unable to join us for he had done as much as anyone in the discovery. The day was fine, the rocks warm and all went well. Fred Botterill led us throughout and as he had now been over most of the ground three times there was not much hesitation. After passing the top of the buttress the climb seemed to me to be the steepest of the height I had been on, but it was satisfactory to find many good belay pins and little resting places. Twice the leader has to run out 80 feet, the second time over the piece where Dr. Taylor found the way, which is very stiff indeed.

I was foolish enough to take a camera with me, but the finest views were in momentary glances, whilst passing over places where both hands are needed for other things than photography, and when a ledge was reached and Fred Botterill looked after the rope for a minute while I pointed the lens down at his brother and Dr. Taylor, exertion and excitement made me tremble too much to get good pictures. But if the climbing interfered with good photography the camera interfered still more with good climbing. Some friends meanwhile had been photographing the rock from below with more success, and as we reached the summit of the Low Man they gave a cheer and hurried back to dinner while we went on our way rejoicing to the Pillar top.

This was my day of days on the Pillar—the fullest of the delights that the climber alone can enjoy in their fulness, but there are other lesser joys which make me look back with pleasure on many a day spent there in sketching, photographing or merely rambling lazily round the rock.   I remember the delight of seeing it one fresh June morning soon after sunrise, with a flood of light on its Northern face, usually so dark and threatening, but the most memorable non-climbing visit to the Pillar was on a day of departure for home, when at breakfast time most men thought the outlook hopeless.   The clouds were thick and not 100 feet from the ground. There was an indefinable look about them, however, which made me feel sure of a grand day, and while the rest of the party sauntered down to catch the train I set off for the Pillar with a camera.   The clouds rose steadily as I went on, keeping always about 100 feet above me and I raced along the High Level track to be at the rock as they were clearing off it.   But though they gradually rose from all the hillsides round, until the sun shone on High Stile and down Ennerdale to the sea, the Pillar remained shrouded.   Time after time a rift would tantalizingly reveal a glimpse of the dark mass and then close. At last, after waiting for two long hours, the clouds began to draw together and for ten minutes I had the grandest views of the rock which I have ever had the luck to get.   For once I was fairly pleased with my photograph, but the reality was beyond all description in its solemnity of rock and delicacy of veiling cloud-wreath through which the sunlight filtered. Each fresh combination of cloud and rock seemed more beautiful than the last until in a moment the Pillar stood bare, the mist and the enchantment were gone, and I fled precipitately to catch my train.

Luckily the enchantment of that and many and many another day there remains in remembrance, but alas, reading over this description now that I have finished writing reminds me of the lifting of those clouds wreaths. There are all the commonplace facts—the footholds and handholds—standing out unromantically in broad daylight, but the accompaniments of good-fellowship, and the glories of wild nature, and the thrill, not of having conquered but of conquering, or at least of fighting —these I cannot hope to convey.

GRASMERE IN WINTER

THE POOL IN THE DALE

VIII. A MEMORIAL SERVICE.

DIMMED and distorted by the small diamond panes
of the East window, but still bright, the snows on
Fairfield's lower slopes gleamed in the wintry sunshine between gaunt interlacing boughs in the
churchyard, as we sat, the first-comers, waiting for
the service in memory of our dead Queen.
Accustomed to summer opulence of leafage shutting
out the distant view I felt a loneliness, as when some
old friend meets us, after absence, with a changed
outlook on the world, and we feel out of touch, not
knowing the links between the mind of yesterday
and of to-day.   On the hills outside I had watched
the slow progress of alternating life and decay and
felt at home amongst them in all their moods, but
there was something discordant here in the vision of
whiteness through the tiny panes.

That large stove too—surely I had never seen it
before, standing so prominently in the middle of
the passage, with its miserable flue, rust-coated for
want of paint or polish, stretching up to the roof
rafters.   It was pleasanter to look restfully on the
well known—the thick rough whitewashed wall
running so curiously down the centre of the church,
pierced by one row over another of rudely shaped
arches, unadorned by capital or moulding;   the

warped beams and stays at all angles above it; the
prim eighteenth-century marble tablets; the quaint
lamps, hanging by long chains from the roof—but
presently the eyes wandered back to the silver light
on the hillside. I wished I were there, tramping
through the crisp upper snows, as we had been
doing an hour or two earlier, when, after some labour
below, where the feet sank deeply in, and one or
two unintentional short and rapid descents higher
up, we had gained a mound commanding the vale.
How beautiful the little village had looked then
through its faint blue haze of smoke, and the sullen
indigo lake, wreathed round by meadows which had
melted their ermine mantles,—all nestling in the
midst of an upper world of whiteness. The trees
on the hillsides no longer groaned beneath a weight
of snow, but frost and cloud had rimed over the
dark green pine boughs or bare purple stems during
the night, and the whiteness seemed only broken by
stone walls on the slopes, and patches of rock here
and there nearer the summits. We had gazed long,
but after a while black figures, by twos and threes,
in the distance, slowly moving from various points
of the compass towards the church had suggested
that we ought to retrace our steps if we wished to
join the gathering, though we left the vision of
beauty needlessly soon, so easy and rapid was the
descent, and the church, after ten minutes of waiting
was still all our own.

Now a brighter gleam of sunlight made Fairfield

sparkle and dissolved the frosted veil thrown over the plantations on its slopes. Had I been alone the attraction might have proved too strong, but my wife and boy were well pleased to rest after their labours, so I continued to look longingly until the arrival of the dalespeople.

The first to fasten attention were two old dames, grey-haired—both a beautiful steely grey—one (the younger, seemingly,) bent and doddering, with puffy cheeks and blinking watery eyes, a type of decrepit old age; the other bearing her years nobly, standing erect throughout the Psalms and hymns while her companion sat limp and vacant. She might have been Wordsworth's 'Lucy' preserved from her untimely death. A far-off murmuring of the becks amongst the mountain stillness seemed imprinted on her features—mouth that still smiled softly, spite of the jaw's collapse; gentle steadfast eyes, that looked beyond the clergyman, beyond the landscape outside, yet not vacantly, but as if fixed on visions of the past. Many times during the service my eyes and thoughts wandered towards her calm face looking out from an old-fashioned purple and grey knitted hood, the only colour in a sea of 'customary black' until the arrival of some scarlet volunteers. Before church-time these latter were somewhere about the village, struggling with trumpets which made a fearful discord with the slow mellow bells above us.

A fat little body, redolent of cheese and greasy

ha'pence, walked up and down the passage, by turns obsequious and officious. While his services were not required he warmed his back at the stove and the two looked a pair singularly harmonious with one another and out of keeping with everything round them. He spied one of the gentry entering and beckoned him forward with a jerk of the head; but the old *roué* left him to wander to the front seats unaccompanied, and, drawing himself up, bowed his demure rustling ladies into the pew before us. The little shopkeeper's face was a picture worth studying for complexity of expression when he turned round to wave his charge to a seat and found himself alone, but he relieved his feelings on some whispering children. Meanwhile, the originator of his confusion seemed in a far from amiable mood. For the most part all I saw was a high collar, and hair parted in the centre right down to it and brushed furiously forward above the ears, but now and then as he glared round, I caught a glimpse of thundery brows and raised nostrils and heard an occasional snort of disapproval—or was it con-tempt?—as though he wished it to be understood that nothing but loyal respect for his Queen would have induced *him* to be there.

The seats were now being rapidly filled, chiefly by ladies, whose sombre attire, though not beautiful, was in some ways a pleasant change from the rival millinery displays of the summer season. How much more restful and thoughtful too, were the faces of these dalespeople than those of the shallow flashy majority of the intruding summer crowd: they made me feel that we were ourselves intruders —probably the only ones.

The noise of trumpets drew nearer and stopped: then a clattering of feet in the porch, and rhythmic thud along the matted aisle as the soldiers marched in, followed by most of the male population—farm labourers, uneasy in black coats, who at their task move with a sort of clumsy dignity; grizzled shepherds, gathered together from remote corners of the valley; healthy, stupid-looking lads who somehow grow into finely-featured men. It was a pleasure to see from the faces in the full church that Lakeland is not yet given over to the tourist and those who depend on him—that the old life still goes on.

The clergy and choir entered and a stillness succeeded, followed by the solemn opening sentences of the Burial Service. Questionings and misgivings, old as the race, rise, almost perforce, in this atmosphere of death's mystery and make it eerie to listen to the plaintive voices of the choir-children chanting words too deep for them to grasp —outpourings of emotion gained in hard experience —alternating confidence, despair and passionate supplication.

> " Lord Thou hast been our refuge : from one
>   generation to another
>   Before the mountains were brought forth, or
>   ever the earth and the world were made :
>   Thou art God,"

and the heart echoed the mighty roll of the simple words.

"Turn Thee again O Lord at the last : and be
    gracious unto Thy servants.
O satisfy us with Thy mercy."

Confidence seemed to spring from merely repeating the strong expression of desire, such power is there in impassioned utterance, and the heart leaped gladly in accord with the final outburst of praise.

How did that string snap and spoil the harmony when the Psalm ended and the lesson began? The clergyman read earnestly, but his conviction had no power to convince. St. Paul's arguments for a life after death only stirred up discord : an inner voice protested "This cold attempt to place reason uppermost has spoilt all; let me command and I will satisfy the heart's desire." Reply came quickly "Spoilt? and deservedly! How often have you prayed 'Lighten our darkness' and here you are wilfully surrounding yourself with the stained glass of childhood's belief—allowing rich pictures of all you long for to intercept the searching light." The heart sank, oppressed : every sentence seemed addressed to reason and yet an insult to the faculty. Feeling lay dormant : to it no appeal was made, until at last, when the clergyman read out "What advantageth it me if the dead rise not? Let us eat and drink for to-morrow we die." Then heart and mind stood together in rebellious indignation. I looked at the clergyman : his face was a denial of what he read; so was that of the old lady in the grey and purple worsted bonnet. Would she not have chosen the good because she felt it to be good and without ulterior aim? Ay, surely, and many another in that church. I wished I were away in the purer air : the dimming and distorting effect of the window panes on the hills and sunshine seemed symbolic. Religion here appeared now to oppress rather than uplift; the atmosphere was tainted with repression and abnegation—one in which weakness might thrive and weariness find solace, but which gave no strength to the strong. On the morrow—Sunday—we would go to a church of a different kind. . . .

Above the dull, grey morning mists, which lay along the valleys, the air was clear and exhilarating, and my youngster struggled bravely through the thick snow over the Kirkstone, wondering at the fairy world around—the ice-curtains hanging over the shining rocks on Red Screes high above us, ever and again veiled by thin white clouds which formed and dissolved as we watched them, softening the blue of the sky above and giving a suggestion of Alpine vastness to the hills whose summits they obscured. As the clouds wandered, patches of dazzling sunlight crossed our path and luminous blue or purple shadows started up as if called by magic along the crisp edges of wind-driven snow billows, disappearing again as the sunlight crossed the level and climbed the opposite fell-side.

Higher up Ill Bell came into view, transformed from a commonplace plebeian hill into a monarch. Shining mists robed it round and glistening snow-fields on its flanks looked in the Turnerian light like glaciers descending towards the verdant pastures of Troutbeck. Life was pure joy. Morning greyness had passed away. Below all was gladness: the lake sparkled; firs and pines rejoiced in the sun, more brilliant green for their late white mantle : in the distance every detail stood out distinctly—there on Pavey Ark was Jack's Rake slanting across the cliff and those scenes of so much enjoyment, the Great and Little Gullies, Rake End Chimney and Gwynne's, all clearly visible eight or nine miles away. What buoyant, invigorating air! A better church, this, than the one in the valley, and a more inspiring. Here life was no dream-like interlude between two eternities—no pilgrimage through a dreary wilderness towards some heavenly home : it was joy, reality, consciousness (so far as limitations would allow) of the vaster all-enfolding spirit. Here was nothing jarring or discordant—here were surroundings which uplifted and helped to a communion with the Being Whom to know is life, "Whose service is perfect freedom." Up here there was no temptation to glory in weakness because we were weak : rather a delight in such slight strength of body and spirit as we had; a burning desire to intensify by exercise all the faculties with which we had been endowed—passions, high and low, no less than wisdom to direct and will to control them—physical endowments as well as mental. The beautiful spirit of renunciation in the little church down in the valley, a spirit so hallowed by associations, what was it but a step towards Nirvana? Emptying the soul of all passion and desire might lead to calm, but what a gulf between it—the calm of death—and a god-like tranquillity which the strongest passions, wisely directed, could not disturb. I hungered here for the virility of great souls—body healthy, perfect; mind full of alertness and fire; sympathising with· us weaker ones without praising or encouraging our weakness—their faculties ever eager for combat.

> " Winds blow and waters roll!
> Strength to the brave and power and deity."

A few hours later the pageant had faded. " Twilight and evening bell " succeeded, bringing with them for a moment the usual harking back towards early faiths, a mood easily disturbed, however, for as we left Lakeland, lying silent and ghostly, " visited all night by troops of stars," the hills seemed themselves looking up towards the pale gleaming lights, each questioning like Heine's youth:

" Oh, solve me the Riddle of life,
  That harrowing, world-old riddle . . .
  Tell me—what signifies man?
  Whence has he come? whither goes he? . ."
  The waves murmur their endless babble,
  The wind blows and the clouds wander,
  The stars glitter coldly indifferent—
  And a fool waits for an answer.

But the mind's vision was once again dimmed and
distorted, this time by the thought of travel-weariness
with a smoke-fouled city as the goal.

PACK-HORSE BRIDGE & MOSEDALE

IX. HASKETT GULLY.

IT was getting towards the end of our Easter holiday at Buttermere, and I had still not wormed out of Haskett-Smith the whereabouts of a good new climb which he and Tucker had discovered two years before, and which we were to go, see and conquer, if fortune favoured. Tucker was under orders, and always referred discreetly to going " yonder," and when I asked point blank where this mysterious place was, Haskett-Smith replied : " In an Edinburgh street—no, the climb is not there—a Scottish nobleman and a beggar were once surprised to see a halfpenny lying in the gutter. It was so unusual a sight that they were both held bound, in amazement, for one second, but the next they both simultaneously darted forward. The nobleman, by virtue of his superior agility, secured the prize, and the beggar, arriving a fraction of a second too late, bared his head and held out his hand, hoping to receive the treasure as a gift. The nobleman, after putting the coin into his pocket, said com-passionately, ' Puir maun ! may the Lord help ye to fin a bawbee for yersel !' Now, sir, you are a good hand at finding bawbees—deny it, if you dare—and they are getting too scarce to be scattered about freely—but come, I'll give you an inkling. It's Black Combe way."

I hazarded the Steeple, but could not get my guess confirmed or denied.

We set off on a brilliant morning, in the direction of Scale Force, skirted the hillside above it and then across Gale Fell and down to Gillerthwaite. Then we crossed the Liza and struck up the little ravine of Low Beck. After following the stream up for a mile or more on to the open moorland, a fine crag came into sight at the head of the valley, with a striking gully in the centre, and to the right of it a huge cleft of the kind which usually looks very fierce and turns out to be a walk up. I took a photograph, but as the light was behind the crag I hoped to secure a better one on our way back, when the sun would have got round on to the rock.

" You have great faith in your powers if you hope to be back here from Black Combe before sunset," remarked Haskett-Smith, but I said that I would be content with this bawbee and leave the Black Combe one for him.

" Well, as Oppenheimer is so struck with this, what do you say, Tucker, just to humour him, shall we take this little thing on the way? A trifle more or less is nothing to a stout Cornishman like you."

The first hundred feet was just a steep vegetable climb; then came an awkward ten feet up a greasy slab which led us into a deep cave, and there we gathered together to consider the next pitch, which looked a serious one. There was only one possible way out of the cave, and that was to work upwards and outwards on the left wall, which was singularly destitute of holds. The floor of the cave was very sloping and bad to stand on, so Tucker anchored himself firmly high up in it and held both of us in, while I gave Haskett-Smith a shoulder. He did not find anything much to pull up by, and called for the ice-axe to try what sort of ledges there might be above.

"Give me the 'escarbadientes,' or I suppose I ought to say ' palito,'" for at breakfast-time Craig had been speaking about the coarseness of the English word 'toothpick' and its Spanish equivalent, and enlarging on the superior politeness of the Portuguese language. "' Palito '—' piolet '—or 'piolito' would perhaps be a more suggestive 'portmanteau' word," said Haskett-Smith, but his philological ingenuity did not help him to find the holds, and we had to resort to ingenuity of another kind.

We passed a loop of rope over a chockstone near the mouth of the cave, and by dint of a pretty free use of one another's shoulders, and of the loop, first as a handhold and later on as a stirrup, Haskett-Smith and I got over the pitch. It was a couple of hours before we managed it, and in the middle of the final effort we were suddenly sensible of a change. While we were lunching beside Low Beck, in brilliant sunshine, a curious leaden haze lay over the coast. I thought it must be smoke drifting over from Barrow, but Haskett-Smith feared it meant bad weather, and now it had come. Snowflakes called our attention back to the world outside, from which the semblance of early summer had fled before the whitening breath of the North. Faster and faster the snow came, and meanwhile Tucker was struggling to get out of his sheltered cave.

" I'm afraid I can't manage this without a shoulder."

" Would you like to test the strength of the rope?"

" Well, I'm in doubt : I would rather not if it can be avoided."

" Do you mean that you would rather not be in doubt, or that you would rather not be in suspense?" asked Haskett-Smith.

" I wish he would be quick : my hands are getting purple with cold."

" Oh, indeed ! I thought you wore them purple to set off your fine linen."

" Ay, you may well be satirical about my clothes. I apologize for the disgraceful state of my jacket— it has been discarded once, but my other was too wet to put on to-day."

" You must have forgotten what trumps were when you discarded that. Ha ! whom have we here? Mr. Tucker, I believe. What changes have come over the world since we three last met ! Alas, that we must so soon part," for before Tucker had fully recovered his wind after the exertions of the pitch, Haskett-Smith was backing up a short chimney above our heads, and his chaff ceased for a while. From the top of the chimney he shouted down, " The bawbee is ours, if you lose no time. This is where we got down to a couple of years ago, Tucker."

Above the chimney there was a corner which required careful balance, and both in this pitch and the remainder of the climb the snow, which had to be cleared from handholds, added greatly to the difficulties.

There was no cairn building at the top. We plunged down an easy gully, and hurriedly despatched our remaining provisions, including a thermal bottle full of hot soup, which proved more acceptable than we had anticipated when packing the rücksack. Our tramp back to Buttermere was a continuous struggle against the wind and driving snow, which fell all night and produced an elfin world of whiteness for the sun to shine upon next day.

Some discussion arose later on as to the position of the climb. Haskett-Smith said that it was on the north side of Scoat Fell at the end nearest Haycock, but I think this was because Tucker and I had christened the climb Haskett Gully, and he was anxious to make people believe that the name was really nothing more than a euphonised form of " Hay-Scoat." I held that it was at the end of Scoat Fell nearest Steeple, and that the crag was indicated by the striking projection in the 2,500 ft.

contour line above the source of Low Beck. We
settled the question the following Whit-Sunday,
when Messrs. Haskett-Smith, Eric Greenwood,
W. A. Brigg and I made the second ascent, but I
was not allowed to take any credit for my guess.
After a cairn had been built and the bearings of the
crag top inspected, Haskett-Smith struck an attitude,
and, addressing me, said : " My dear sir, little as you
may imagine it, you have stumbled upon the truth :
what you propounded in jest, as the most unlikely
place you could think of, turns out to be no other
than the actual spot."

The best base for the climb is Wastdale Head,
whence it can be reached in a couple of hours by
going up Mosedale past the Y boulder and following
up the stream which comes down between Red Pike
and Scoat Fell until some striking slabs are reached,
high up in a wild lonely hollow. Then cross Scoat
Fell and make for the narrow neck between it and
Steeple, from the lowest point of which a sharp
descent leads to the foot of the crag.

X. CASTLES IN THE AIR

As I sit by the fireside, with good maps (those most wonderful quickeners of memory and imagination) spread round me, luxuriating in the rival enticements of first one and then another of the Lakeland valleys as a fit spot for retirement, an evening's chat long ago comes across my reverie. A friend, with whom we had been enjoying a farewell climb before his departure for the other side of the globe, was sportively forecasting.

"Well," he remarked, "spite of good luck calling me so far off, from a place I love to one in some ways even better, I'll wager five pounds that I have a house here before any of you. At least—no, I won't do that, either; I'll make it shillings, or one of you'll be taking some bit of a cottage for a fiver, while I'm away, just for the fun of beating me."

"Done! I don't believe you'll ever be able to afford retirement. As long as I've known you your wants have always been ahead of your income. Do you remember the early times when we always tramped over the hills from the station to some far away little farmhouse, with as much as we could carry in our knapsacks? A fine contrast to this coming in lordly fashion to the best hotel, and to our climax of effeminate extravagance to-day in taking a carriage and pair to our climb!"

"Wasn't it ripping? You ought to have been on the box with me, and seen the way the horses enjoyed it, and leaned your head on one side as a branch of crackly red gold leaves brushed past. Simply ripping! and a good dinner, with drinkable wine after our exertions, and now comfortable chairs and good cigars and good coffee. No, I don't ask for much, but I like it of the best. Still, I am keen on some day having an unpretentious old place embowered in trees, with windows towards the setting sun; yes, and overlooking some peaceful water—we'll say the south end of Windermere—where I can 'feed this mind of ours in a wise passiveness.' But do you think I'm going to stint myself and be miserable now, for the sake of possible pleasures later on? Not I!"

"Hello, hello, hello!" interjected one of two very contentious angling friends who happened to be in the smoke-room at the time : "Follow that scent along a bit! I've been trying all day to convince this exasperatingly self-opinioned old pal of mine to pack up his rods and come off with me to Scotland to some place where we might have some chance of catching fish; and just because the three weeks he'd arranged for beforehand is up to-morrow, to-morrow he must off at the call of duty—damn it—and deny himself a bit of sport he's just longing for. 'Pig-headedness,' I call it! And no need, like I have, every now and then to stop the fun and run to earth until fresh dividends come in—although heaven knows when I'm cooped up for want of funds I generally get into mischief twice as costly as having a gay time. But I'm a damned fool to try to persuade him."

" Barring the adjective, I quite agree," added the other fisherman.

" Damn the adjective! You're too deuced particular, you are."

"Admitted (barring the adverbs this time), and I'm particularly particular about enjoyment. I like to get the full flavour of everything, and I find that freedom and fresh air are doubly delightful after the discipline of routine, and give a relish in their turn to the struggle of brain against brain."

" Ay," said one of our climbing party, " I quite agree with you, but I'm going to encourage these two silly friends of mine. I hope you'll both make your fortunes in the next year or two, and ask us up here every week-end. Let me see, the south end of Windermere is your foolish fancy? yes? and yours?"

" Somewhere near Derwentwater will do well enough for me."

" Dear me! you're both very inconsiderate for your mountaineering friends. Now, can't I persuade either of you gentlemen to reconsider your decisions, and settle in the heart of things? You see, if you set up a motor, your distance from a station would be no inconvenience to us, so don't let that stand in the way."

" Thanks awfully for your consideration."

" Don't mention it, old chap! Here's another little suggestion that might be of service to you when you're afraid of any of us staying too long. Instead of invitations send return tickets—available for the week-end to mere acquaintances, friends honoured with a double week-end, and members of the brotherhood with the delicate attention of tourist tickets."

" We shall send you a day excursion when the time comes."

" In that case I shall feel bound for the honour of our friendship to lose the return half. But to revert, why the south end of Windermere?"

" For peace, my boy, and freedom from tourists, the soothing effect of lonely wooded hills and restful water, with nothing grand enough for guide books to gush over. It would exasperate me to live constantly with your theatrical scenery, looking as if it had been prepared to make people open their eyes with 'admiration not unmixed with awe'—that's the proper phrase, isn't it? If I had a house in Hollow Stones I should just swear at all the sublimities after a week or two. No! I want visions of our old haunts far away amongst the sunset clouds, to tempt me off the next morning, and many a jolly day we'll have there together yet."

" It's my opinion," said the undemonstrative angler, " that any place would soon get wearisome if retirement bound you largely to it;" and the thought of this brings me back suddenly to the advantages of "castles in the air," built by the fireside at the inspiration of maps and happy memories. Do inconveniences about the selected site obtrude?—the unsubstantial fabric is forthwith transported to a more desired haven. Is there a whispering suspicion that the amenities of Derwentwater may be profaned, as those of parts of Windermere have been, by the occasional dumping of trippers?—The mind unconsciously withdraws to more secluded ground. It reverts to places like Fell Foot, in Little Langdale, where the cuckoos answering from hill to hill and lambs bleating below are the chief disturbers of the early summer stillness; or Gatesgarth, above Buttermere, with its grave silent beauty; or Thorneythwaite or Butterilkel. But the advantages of nearness to Keswick remain—the social intercourse, the convenience for visits from distant friends, the many desirabilities which appeal most to the female portion of the household, are all fixed too firmly in the mind to be displaced by a mere alteration of site; they are transported with the castle. And in ways like this our harbour of refuge has become by degrees a compound of the desires of years.

It is an old house, for the risk of injuring the look of the country round with a new building was too great. It is built of the many-shaded greeny-blue slate which harmonises so well with Lakeland surroundings, but the southern side is covered with cream-washed rough-cast, which, seen against the background of dark trees that shelter and partly overhang the house, has often been a welcome landmark to friends returning at twilight. The porch is open, with stone seats on either side, embowered in a wild tangle of rose and honeysuckle. The chimneys are of true Lake-district pattern—square below and round above, with a sort of child's card-house of slates on the top. No extensive alteration had to be made externally, except the removal of an outhouse which seemed to have been placed right opposite the best windows with the special purpose of hiding the glorious view towards the grander mountains at the head of Borrowdale. There is no proper garden—the creepers and some old-fashioned flowers close up to the house are all that need attention, as the cluster of trees to the north and a small lawn where the outhouse was, occupy all our grounds. But we have only to pass through a gate in the wall and we are in grounds more delightful than those of any nobleman's mansion; rough, tangled woods where anemone and primrose, and bluebell follow one another, and up the hillside above through breast-high bracken which flames every autumn amongst the grey lichen-covered rocks. These are my grounds, thanks to the generosity of Lake district owners, mine and anyone else's who likes to enjoy them.

I wander on and on without hindrance. Wherever I want most to go is free to me. I climb up above the bracken, with a new combination of the lake and mountains to wonder at whenever a pause seems pleasantest, until I am on an airy ridge which entices on to the very heart of the mountain wildness. Nor is the spot wanting in softer charms. In a ravine above the house a stream comes exultingly down, and not far away is the bathing pool amongst the trees, though not hidden from the sunshine which strikes through the clear deep water—a pool combining the beauties of that in the little gorge where Langstrath meets Greenup and the many in Upper Eskdale above Throstle Garth. The dazzling spray which comes over the barrier above the pool's smooth basin rises from the turbulence in a turquoise foam of bursting bubbles : from turquoise the water clears to sparkling emerald, and then passes into still dark depths which are a temptation to any swimmer.

" But your house seems to me to be on both sides of Derwentwater at once, and there are no pools like that at Langstrath so near to Keswick as your description seems to indicate," says a knowing one, " and——"

No! you foolishly accurate person, you are probably right, and when the long-looked-for time of retirement comes I shall not be able to discover the house where these delights are brought together. But it is not the place where I shall then live that I have been describing; it is the house in which I am living at present—in my dreams. From it I undertake long mountain rambles and make new climbs, regardless of the fact that in all probability I shall be too old and stiff. There in my ample leisure I paint pictures which are not rejected by unfeeling hanging committees for "want of space," as are those done in spare moments now. Hundreds of half-known nooks are explored. Books that have long been on my list for reading are at last enjoyed.

Will the capacity for enjoyment have passed, as with so many who have achieved their desire by toiling and scheming until the gathering of riches has in itself become life's supremest pleasure? Perchance—but at least to-day is mine. I enjoy more than ever the delights which Lakeland bestows during my all-too-brief holidays, and year by year my castle in the air acquires not only more entrancing possibilities, but also the clearer definition of a not-quite-so-distant prospect.

So I continue to doze by the fire, thinking of what may never come to pass, and deriving fresh inspiration by occasional reference to the outspread map, with its pregnant network of lines and dots and thought-quickening names.

XI. ANTICIPATIONS.

Ah, Love! could you and I with Him conspire
To grasp this sorry scheme of things entire,
    Would not we shatter it to bits—and then
Re-mould it nearer to the heart's desire?
                                —*Omar Khayyám*.

ONE of the pleasantest diversions after a hard day
on the hills is to sit in the Wastdale smoke-room
listening to the endless stream of conversation,
argument and banter which flows on, now with
smooth serenity, now uproariously tossed from side
to side, until thoughts of fitness for the morrow
warn one after another to slink off bedwards.   The
room is small and has seat accommodation for about
half-a-dozen, but this only gives the more opportunity for assuming unconventional postures on the
floor.   To-night the score of men who are thickening
the atmosphere, are careless about bedtime, for the
morrow is the day of dispersion.   In the place of
honour, by the fire, as of right, sits the Wanderer,
listening for the most part, with an amused, tolerant
expression playing round his grizzled moustache and
beard, but breaking out at times into the most
dogmatic and unaccommodating dicta.   Then his
face becomes full of serious animation and forms
a fine contrast to the assumed nonchalance of the
Bohemian beside him, or the more youthful

animation of the majority in the room, but just now he is puffing quietly at his favourite down-curved pipe, waiting to be roused.

" May one inquire what last villainy has been perpetrated?" the Bohemian asks, holding out a hand for the climbing book, in which a youth has just finished entering the record of some exploit. " Have you violated the virginity of some secret cleft, or has 'the attempt and not the deed confounded?' Hm!—threading the rope,—a shoulder up once more—are we to consider that conforming to the rules of the game, umpire?" he continues, addressing the Wanderer.

" In my improved system of mountaineering," replies the latter, " all aid, whether human or artificial, is absolutely forbidden in any circumstances whatever, and the offender is condemned to be hauled, between two guides, up Alps, provided with fixed ropes and spikes. The more a climber depends on his own brain and muscle the better, and the sooner you stop standing on each other's heads and shoulders, and using artificial aids on the rocks, the less chance there is that you will be made fools of by a few professional gymnasts and engineers."

" Well, I, for one, don't agree with you at all. I think one of the great pleasures of our sport is the good fellowship which comes from feeling that the climb is being done by the party rather than by the individual members of it."

" Oh, I can imagine the undying gratitude that

each feels for all the never-to-be-mentioned pulls and shoves from his companions. No, the essential element in mountaineering, as a sport, is the over-coming of difficulties; in proportion as they are evaded the sport diminishes, and the ideal moun-taineer is the man who makes first ascents, alone and unaided."

" Hear, hear!" a young Yorkshireman chimes in; " step up one, Wanderer. I'll go nap on those sentiments;" but the Wanderer doesn't seem quite pleased, and remarks to the Bohemian : " ' Preserve me from my friends; I can defend myself against my enemies.' "

Meanwhile the Yorkshireman chatters on : " Look at the first ascents of the Needle and Pinnacle. Talk about pulling big trees up, there are trump cards for you. For rattling good sport unroped climbing is A1."

A milder man now joins in the conversation. "Well, if you won't take proper precautions for your own sakes, I think you might for the sake of others. Don't all the leading authorities on climbing insist on the use of the rope?"

The Wanderer fires up. " ' Sake of others!' 'Authorities!' What are authorities? Humbugs, sir; for the most part, humbugs—the concentrated essence of ineptitude! Good of others, indeed! You are just as short-sighted in your altruism as the rest of the civilised world, that saves up all its weaklings in hospitals to propagate a debilitated race, and makes conventional hypocrites of its worthless members, instead of encouraging them to dare to be themselves. If they only committed their crimes and were hanged, future generations might be saved from their leaven; and so with you and your rope. If you are anxious for the good of society, why, in the name of all reasonableness, don't you go unroped? If you're a duffer, and fall and kill yourself, the world will be well rid of you, and you won't run the risk of dragging down a man the world's in need of."

·" Those are surely very un-Christian sentiments," replies the other.

" Modernity," the Bohemian remarks.

" But," the milder man adds, " why do you yourself always go roped if those are your opinions?"

" Mine? Not in the least," answers the Wanderer. "I'm a Hedonist. I've not been advocating altruism. They are yours, all ·of yours, taken to a logical conclusion."

" Rats!" ejaculated the Yorkshireman, emphatically.

" I beg your pardon! I don't quite grasp the drift of your remark—or argument, shall I say?"

" I mean they're not mine, anyhow; and if that's your tack, by Jove, I'm not having any."

" If that's what you mean, your terse and original manner of expressing it in some measure atones for the occult contradiction——"

" Here, I say, steady on! Keep smiling! I've not learnt double Dutch."

" Don't overstrain him, old boy," says one who, tired of lying in what looked an easy attitude against another man's shins, had got up to stretch himself and glance outside, " if you want to make any improvements leave the sport and begin with the weather. We shall have a soaker on the way home to-morrow; clouds scurrying across from the south-west and the mercury falling."

The Wanderer looks up with a twinkle, remarking, " I intend to make a fortune some day out of an aneroid for sale to hotels and boarding houses—warranted always to rise when tapped; the subsequent fall to be managed stealthily when unobserved. A wetting never harms anyone, but worrying because one expects to get wet plays the very devil with enjoyment."

" I like your calm indifference," says my Tall friend, sitting on the table edge. " I wish you had to walk with us to Windermere, to-morrow, instead of trapping it down to Seascale; we'd see whether you'd sit still in the train with squelchy boots and clammy knees, without swearing, eh, Tommy, lad? Really, the railway ought to be brought up here to take us back from our climbing in comfort.

" Shame, shame," resounds on all sides.

" If there's one thing I detest it's getting wet on the way home. Now a short line from Drigg is all that's wanted, or you might have a delightful run from Windermere to Ambleside, right up Langdale (no one can say that it's not spoilt already with those messy quarries), and a tunnel through to Wastdale Head."

"I might lose my chair if I got up to kick him," says the Wanderer, "but perhaps someone else will oblige," and the Bohemian is stirred to prophesy "Every peak and valley shall be accessible, but the access thereto shall then be of no avail."

"Why not?" the Wanderer asks; "won't any places spring up for the greasy multitudes to get beer at? Besides, you don't consider that though there would be nothing for them to look at but scenery, they would have the satisfaction of annihilating the monopoly enjoyed by the few who come here at present."

"Nay," says another, "you're too hard on the poor fellows; I'm sure that each of us in his time has met all conditions of men on the hills, and almost all of them appreciative."

"An argument on the other side," remarks the Wanderer. "The obstacles in the way of reaching the best mountains at present weed out the un-appreciative. The only advantage that I can see in an express service to Wastdale is that there would probably be also an express service from it, by which we could quickly rush away from the invaders and solace ourselves with recollections."

"The memory of what has been and nevermore will be," the Bohemian adds, to himself.

"Ay, you may sneer," the Tall Man continues, "but I shall stick up for the rights of the masses in

spite of you all. We had to endure enough
conservatism and bunkum—pig-headed sentimen-
talism—from every pottering busybody before the
Thirlmere scheme was passed, and now look at the
thousands who enjoy the lake on a first-rate road,
and have the pleasure of knowing that the silver
threads coursing down Helvellyn are supplying a
million people with pure mountain water."

"Do you remember what Thirlmere used to look
like?" asks another, and being answered in the
negative, continues: "Well, your finely engineered
road, with its monotonous wall, used to be on one
side a picturesque highway, and on the other a
delightful rough lane, which kept the few cyclists
there were well away. Lovely, irregular, moss-
covered walls, with wild geranium in the crannies
and crowned with ferns instead of a mean railing;
and the walk, too, diversified by streams brawling
down the hillside, by which you could loiter and
drink; now all tantalisingly culverted and kept out
of reach, and the monotony of the wall to-day is
chiefly relieved by cast-iron gates——"

"Painted a delicate duck-egg blue."

"Admitted—blue cast-iron gates, and notices as
to the penalty for stealing water. Why, merely to
have seen the beauty of Thirlmere's old outline from
Raven Crag and the quaint bridge that crossed it at
Armboth would have convinced you."

"Nay, man, man! the shape's beautiful enough
for anyone as it is, and as for the wall, never fear

it'll get as rickety as the old one in time, and as much in need of being cleared of weeds, if that's all you want."

" Is it a fact," asks a man in the corner, playing chess under difficulties, " that the 'rock of names' has been tampered with?"

" That's a very minor matter," the Bohemian replies; " they've got a new one—beautiful polished granite with the noble appellations of the Waterworks Committee blazoned thereon in gold, and set up on a sham castle, which covers over the ugliness and horror of Manchester's new throat—a sham castle, with sham loopholes, sham machicolations and a plentiful array of senseless battlements."

" Well," the Tall Man retorts, " at least they're the names of decent, respectable citizens, and as for Coleridge and Wordsworth, they were a couple of old vandals to carve their initials on the scenery. I wonder what the inhabitants said when they and Southey pounced down here and started exploiting the district? I'll bet they spoke about it exactly as you're talking now about the improvements of to-day. If you'd lived a hundred years ago you would all have protested—every stick-in-the-mud of you—against Wordsworth for dragging the beauties of these sequestered dales out of their retirement, and leading a horde of outlandish literary gents and tourists to overrun the district; but because the damage was done before your day you admire it. It's always the same. I'll warrant there were fine outcries before Grasmere Church was set up, letters to the *Times*, Mountain-solitude Preservation Societies, Leagues against interference with 'immemorial rights of rapine.' Ay, and now it gives the keynote of peace to this most tranquil vale, according to the writer of descriptive papers, full of umbrageous and ethereal thingamajigs."

"Well done," chimes in an engineer: "you'll convert them all soon. In the meantime I may state that I am prepared to give estimates for the proposed railway, and I'll stand you a drink, 'Long Legs,' on the strength of it!"

"Eh, man, man, I'm only kidding you. Do you think *I* want any more roads and railways?" This sudden change of front quite upsets the seriousness with which some of the party were trying to approach the question, but the Tall Man continues quite calmly: "Nay, when I become a millionaire I'll buy up the whole of the wild part of the Lake District for the nation,—the Sca Fell and Bow Fell groups, and the mountains round the heads of Ennerdale, Borrowdale, and Langdale—the Old Man group also I would like, but—no, no, I'm afraid Coniston is too much spoilt; the quarries on the Honister might perhaps be cleared away, along with the wire railings on some of the Ennerdale tops, and then we'll have a Trust to see that there are no more railways or sordid industries."

"And all the old shepherds shall be waiters and the farmers' wives and daughters rapacious landladies, eh? And the paths shall be made straight, and finger-posts plentifully supplied, that we may all walk therein. No, I put not my confidence in Trusts, nor my trust in would-be benefactors."

The Wanderer nods assents to the Bohemian's cynical forebodings, and adds despondently: "Trust or no Trust, it will all come to the same thing soon. I saw it happen so at Zermatt before some of you were born, and I foresee the fate of Wastdale Head. A road over the Sty will be the beginning; then there will be an outcry of lack of accommodation, and several well-appointed hotels will naturally follow, with a guide's bureau beside the bandstand and telescopes in the parterres for watching the principal climbs. Next, a funicular railway up Gavel Neese to an Aussichtspunkt Beer-garden on the Gable top, with a station midway for visitors to the Needle and Arêtes. Performances on the Needle might take place at stated times in correspondence with the trains, and for the benefit of those who are doing the Lakes in three days, and can spare no time for any sights, except those marked with a double star, cinematograph exhibitions of ascents would be given in the Wastdale Concert Hall at night. Then, if I might suggest further probable improvements, the best view points on the mountain could be planted with seats (no doubt our friend's Lake District Fund would undertake this), and the various routes on the crags could be indicated by spashes of paint, freshened up annually before the season. Danger-boards at the bottom of certain climbs have already been suggested, I think; on the easier and more frequented it will be necessary to regulate the traffic by confining ascents to one route and descents to another. Then beggars might be licensed to yodel and make horn-echoes in front of precipices for the delectation of visitors."

" Really," the Tall Man strikes in, "when all this comes to pass I shall not be bothered every year by my friends to go to Switzerland with them; they'll find all its advantages here."

" Then, of course, having done all they could think of for the delight of the greatest number the Trustees would naturally wish to do honour to all who had helped to make this possible, by erecting inappropriate monuments in prominent places to our friend the donor, to Wordsworth and Ruskin, to each other, perhaps. I don't know whether any other innovations occur to anyone."

More wild life—red deer and an eagle or two is suggested as an improvement, but a Scotchman fires up at this with : " Some folks don't know when they're well off; na, we've seen what wild life means in Scotland."

" Give our Highland experience, Thomas," says the Tall Man; "they're not always so strict as people imagine."

" No! and I fancy that a considerable proportion of the Scotch ascents are made in prohibited months.

However, we went to a glen where we understood, from the guide-book, that there was no prohibition, although every day we came across 30 or 40 deer and watched them race up the corries in front of us. Well, each morning we passed an old Highlander in his potato patch, with bare-legged kiddies about him, or with his sheep dogs at the foot of the hills, and had the usual word with him on the state of the weather, so when we found him at the Inn with our Host one evening, of course we ordered whisky for him and started to chat. After a while I began to tell of some fine stags we had seen while on the rocks; they couldn't see or scent us, but kept looking about uneasily when we loosened a stone, and we managed to get quite close before they spotted us and dashed off in a panic. Well, old what's his name, the landlord, listened for a while, and then said, drily, " I'm thinking you'd better no' be telling where you've been and what you've been seeing," but the Highlander (who was a keeper, of course) only remarked : 'Ach, maybe they'd pe hares,' and hares, long or short eared, as the case might be, we called them while he remained there."

" Ay," the Tall Man adds, " it was a fine sight, but not worth exchanging for freedom."

" Bother the red deer," interposes an irreverent youth. " I want to know why there are none of the pink and white variety now, as there used to be in Albert Smith's days, to smother us with flowers and kisses on our safe return, or to implore us to rest

our weary heads upon their breasts as they implored
Sir Excelsior. But then, of course, none of us has
the correct sad brow—or is it a falchion eye or
clarion tongue that's wanting?"

While the company is in the vein for improvements I make a venture myself, but it is ruled out
of order, being nothing else than the turning of
Saddleback, so as to link the Helvellyn range with
Skiddaw, block the railway, crush the disfiguring
granite works, and show its almost Alpine ridges to
the heart of Lakeland instead of to the outer world.
Another suggestion is more favourably considered,
for, although it involved the subsidence of south-
west Cumberland to the extent of two or three
hundred feet, instances of similar occurrences are
quickly given, whereas the removal of mountains is
apparently unheard of except as a test of faith. I
draw pictures of the sea submerging the tract between
Blackcombe and Whitehaven, with its mines, railways
and watering places, and reaching up Wastdale as
up some wild Highland loch.

"Tell you how," an American remarks to the fire,
"that's all middling good so far as it goes, but
another submergence seems more pressing—I
indicate the people. You don't give your scenery
a chance. I sit on the top of Sca Fell and try to
locate the objects of interest, when up pop
irrepressible individuals out of chimneys and Lord
knows where all around, until the hillock is all
scabby with fellow-creatures."

"Allow me to shake hands with you," says the Wanderer, "that's the only reasonable suggestion we've had yet," and then he goes on to tell of the pleasures of loneliness; of tent-life in the High Alps away from the throng, of exploration in distant parts of the globe. We stir his recollections and he describes the Alps when they were but half known, passes on to the Himalayas, with side stories of Eastern ways, Gurkha guides, hypnotic jugglers; from there jumping to and fro about the earth and ending, as we began, in Lakeland, but in the days when the wilder parts of it were really lonely, before there were finger-posts on the mountain passes and dress circle seats opposite the Napes Needle; when the gullies and chimneys were unnamed and the cliffs undisturbed save by buzzards and ravens.

The Tall Man told me next day, as we tramped homewards over Sca Fell Pike, that in his sleep a railway porter shook him up and asked for his ticket. "Coniston," he answered drowsily. "Coniston, where's Coniston?" said the porter, but another one heard and replied, "Oh, he's all right; it used to be called that in the old days of the quarries; he means Doe Crag. But he's got no ice-axe. Just get him a rope and ice-axe—you know the Trust regulations since the last accident."

"Oh, man!" he added, longingly, and I fervently agreed, "if only Lakeland could be left for each one of us exactly as he first knew it."